The Evo-Stik
Northern Premier League
Supporters'
Guide
and Yearbook
2012

EDITOR
John Robinson

Second Edition

For details of our range of over 1,900 books and 400 DVDs, visit our web site or contact us using the information shown below.

British Library Cataloguing in Publication Data
A catalogue record for this book is available from the British Library

ISBN: 978-1-86223-222-8

Copyright © 2011, SOCCER BOOKS LIMITED (01472 696226)
72 St. Peter's Avenue, Cleethorpes, N.E. Lincolnshire, DN35 8HU, England
Web site http://www.soccer-books.co.uk
e-mail info@soccer-books.co.uk

Printed and bound in the UK by 4edge Ltd, Hockley.

FOREWORD

The "Supporters' Guide" series of books began life as "The Travelling Supporters' Guide" in 1982 and a separate guide covering the top two tiers of the Non-League pyramid has been published by Soccer Books Limited for almost 20 years! However, this is only the second edition of a Supporters' Guide dealing solely with the Northern Premier League clubs and we hope that it is well received.

We have been unable to visit every ground in the course of preparing this guide and, as a consequence, we have been unable to obtain up-to-date ground photographs for all of the clubs. If any readers wish to send us suitable ground photographs for use in future editions of this guide, please contact us at the address shown on the facing page.

Where we use the term 'Child' for concessionary prices, this is often also the price charged to Senior Citizens.

The fixtures listed later in this book were released just a short time before we went to print and, as such, some of the dates shown may be subject to change. We therefore suggest that readers treat these fixtures as a rough guide and check dates carefully before attending matches.

Finally, we would like to wish our readers a safe and happy spectating season.

John Robinson
EDITOR

ACKNOWLEDGEMENTS

In the 6 months since we embarked upon the preparation of this guide, we have been greatly impressed by the cooperation extended to us by League officials and many individuals within the clubs themselves.

Consequently, our thanks go to the numerous club officials who have aided us in the compilation of information contained in this guide and particularly to Alan Allcock of the Evo-Stik Northern Premier League for his assistance.

Our thanks also go to Michael Robinson (page layouts), Bob Budd (cover artwork), Tony Brown (Cup Statistics – www.soccerdata.com). We would also like to thank:

Chris Bush – footballgroundz.co.uk
David Bauckham – davidbauckham.photoshelter.com
and Martin Wray – www.footballgroundsinfocus.com

for providing a number of the ground photographs used within this guide.

CONTENTS

THE EVO-STIK NORTHERN PREMIER LEAGUE PREMIER DIVISION

Secretary Angie Firth   **Phone** (01422) 410691

Address 23 High Lane, Norton Tower, Halifax HX2 0MW

Web Site evostikleague.pitchero.com

Clubs for the 2011/2012 Season

ASHTON UNITED FC

Founded: 1878
Former Names: Hurst FC and Rose Hill FC
Nickname: 'Robins'
Ground: Hurst Cross, Surrey Street, Ashton-Under-Lyne OL6 8DY
Record Attendance: 11,000 (1952)

Colours: Shirts are Red and White halves, Black shorts
Telephone Nº: (0161) 339-4158
Fax Number: (0161) 339-4158
Ground Capacity: 4,500 **Seating Capacity:** 250
Pitch Size: 110 × 72 yards
Web site: www.ashtonutd.com

GENERAL INFORMATION

Car Parking: Street parking only
Coach Parking: At the ground
Nearest Railway Station: Ashton (1 mile)
Nearest Bus Station: Ashton
Club Shop: At the ground
Opening Times: Before and during matches only
Telephone Nº: (0161) 330-9800

GROUND INFORMATION

Away Supporters' Entrances: No usual segregation

ADMISSION INFO (2011/2012 PRICES)

Adult Standing/Seating: £8.00
Concessionary Standing/Seating: £5.00
Note: One Under-14 admitted free with each paying adult
Programme Price: £1.50

DISABLED INFORMATION

Wheelchairs: Accommodated
Helpers: Please phone the club for information
Prices: Please phone the club for information
Disabled Toilets: Yes
Contact: – (Bookings are not necessary)

Travelling Supporters' Information:
Routes: From the M1: Exit at Juntion 35A and follow signs for Manchester A616. Follow A616 for 11 miles then turn left at roundabout towards Manchester on A628. Follow A638 for 14 miles, passing through Tintwistle and Hollingworth. At the first set of traffic lights at the Gunn Inn go straight on and up the hill for ½ mile. Bear right at the A6018 signposted Ashton-Under-Lyne, Stalybridge and Mossley. Follow for 3 miles, passing Stalybridge Celtic FC on the left. At the 4th set of traffic lights turn right just past the BP Garage. Continue up Ridge Hill Lane for 250 yards where the road bears left and becomes Darnton Road. Continue, passing boating lake and Hospital on the right. Continue through the lights signposted Oldham and go up the hill for ½ mile. * Turn left at the first set of traffic lights then immediately right for the ground; From the M60: Take M60 towards Stockport, exit at Junction 23 and turn left (signposted Ashton). After 100 yards turn right at traffic lights onto A635 towards Ashton. After ½ mile you will reach a roundabout with a Police Station on the left. Stay in the 2nd lane heading towards Stalybridge & Halifax (still A635). Go straight on at next roundabout with Asda on the right until the following roundabout. Take 2nd exit signposted A670 Tameside Hospital. After 500 yards turn right into Mossley Road and after 600 yards turn left at the traffic lights towards Oldham and continue up the hill for ½ mile. Then as from *.

BRADFORD PARK AVENUE FC

Founded: 1907 (Re-formed in 1988)
Former Names: None
Nickname: 'Avenue'
Ground: Horsfall Stadium, Cemetery Road, Bradford, BD6 2NG
Record Attendance: 2,100 (2003)
Pitch Size: 112 × 71 yards

Colours: Green & White striped shirts, White shorts
Telephone Nº: (01274) 604578 (Ground)
Office Number: (01274) 660066
Ground Capacity: 3,000
Seating Capacity: 1,247
Web site: www.bpafc.com

GENERAL INFORMATION

Car Parking: Street parking and some spaces at the ground
Coach Parking: At the ground
Nearest Railway Station: Bradford Interchange (3 miles)
Nearest Bus Station: Bradford Interchange (3 miles)
Club Shop: At the ground
Opening Times: Matchdays only
Telephone Nº: –

GROUND INFORMATION

Away Supporters' Entrances & Sections:
Segregation only used when required

ADMISSION INFO (2011/2012 PRICES)

Adult Seating: £9.00
Senior Citizen/Student Seating: £6.00
Child Standing: £2.00 (£1.00 when with a paying adult)
Programme Price: £2.00

DISABLED INFORMATION

Wheelchairs: Accommodated in front of the Stand
Helpers: Please phone the club for information
Prices: Please phone the club for information
Disabled Toilets: Available
Contact: – (Bookings are not necessary)

Travelling Supporters' Information:
Routes: Exit the M62 at Junction 26 and take the M606 to its end. At the roundabout go along the A6036 (signposted Halifax) and pass Odsal Stadium on the left. At the roundabout by Osdal take the 3rd exit (still A6036 Halifax). After just under 1 mile, turn left at the King's Head pub into Cemetery Road. The ground is 150 yards on the left.

BURSCOUGH FC

Burscough FC are groundsharing with Skelmersdale United during the 2011/2012 season.

Founded: 1946
Former Names: None
Nickname: 'Linnets'
Ground: West Lancashire College Stadium, Stormy Corner, Selby Place, Stanley Industrial Estate, Skelmersdale WN8 8EF
Record Attendance: 4,798 (at Burscough)

Pitch Size: 110 × 70 yards
Colours: Green shirts and shorts
Telephone Nº: (01695) 722123
Fax Number: (01695) 722123
Ground Capacity: 2,300
Seating Capacity: 240
Web site: www.pitchero.com/clubs/burscough

GENERAL INFORMATION

Car Parking: At the ground
Coach Parking: At the ground
Nearest Railway Station: Parbold (4 miles)
Club Shop: At the ground
Opening Times: Matchdays only
Telephone Nº: –

GROUND INFORMATION

Away Supporters' Entrances & Sections:
Segregation only used when required

ADMISSION INFO (2011/2012 PRICES)

Adult Standing/Seating: £9.00
Child/Senior Citizen Standing/Seating: £5.00
Programme Price: £2.00

DISABLED INFORMATION

Wheelchairs: Accommodated
Helpers: Admitted
Prices: Normal prices for the disabled. Helpers are charged concessionary prices
Disabled Toilets: Available
Contact: (01695) 722123 (Bookings are not necessary)

Travelling Supporters' Information:
Routes: Exit the M58 at Junction 4 and head into Skelmersdale. Continue straight on at the roundabout into Glenburn Road then turn left at the next roundabout into Neverstitch Road, following signs for Stanley Industrial Estate. Turn right at the next roundabout into Staveley Road then left into Statham Road. The ground is on the left in Selby Place after 500 yards.

BUXTON FC

Founded: 1877
Former Names: None
Nickname: 'The Bucks'
Ground: The Silverlands, Buxton   SK17 6QH
Record Attendance: 6,000 (1951/52 season)
Pitch Size: 110 × 74 yards

Colours: Royal Blue shirts and shorts
Telephone Nº: (01298) 23197
Ground Capacity: 4,000
Seating Capacity: 490
Web Site: www.buxtonfc.co.uk

GENERAL INFORMATION
Car Parking: Limited number of spaces at the ground
Coach Parking: At the ground
Nearest Railway Station: Buxton (¾ mile)
Club Shop: At the ground
Opening Times: Matchdays only
Telephone Nº: –

GROUND INFORMATION
Away Supporters' Entrances & Sections:
No usual segregation

ADMISSION INFO (2011/2012 PRICES)
Adult Standing/Seating: £9.00
Concessionary Standing/Seating: £6.00
Under-16s Standing/Seating: £2.00 (Free when accompanied by a paying adult)
Programme Price: £1.50

DISABLED INFORMATION
Wheelchairs: Accommodated
Helpers: Admitted
Prices: Normal prices apply for the disabled and helpers
Disabled Toilets: Available
Contact: (01298) 23197   (Bookings are not necessary)

Travelling Supporters' Information:
Routes: From Matlock/Bakewell: Take the A6 to Buxton then turn left at the roundabout by Safeway onto the B5059 (signposted Poole's Cavern). Take the first right into Peveril Road, turn left at the T-junction into Cliff Mill and continue into Clifton Road. Turn right at the T-junction into Silverlands and the ground is on the right; From Leek/Macclesfield: Take the A53 to Buxton and turn right onto the B5059 Macclesfield Road at the edge of town. Continue along the B5059, crossing the A515 into Dale Road (still B5059), then take the 6th turning on the left into Peveril Road. Then as above; From Manchester: Take the A6 to Buxton, turn left at the mini-roundabout junction with the A53 continuing up the A6 Bakewell Road. Turn right at the mini-roundabout by Safeway into B5059 Dale Road. Then as above.

CHASETOWN FC |

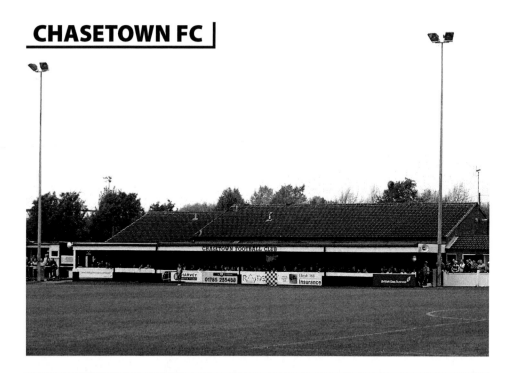

Founded: 1954
Former Names: Chase Terrace Old Scholars FC
Nickname: 'The Scholars'
Ground: The Scholars Ground, Church Street, Chasetown, Burntwood   WS7 3QL
Record Attendance: 2,134 (2005/06 season)
Pitch Size: 111 × 71 yards

Colours: Royal Blue shirts and shorts
Telephone Nº: (01543) 682222
Fax Number: (01543) 684609
Ground Capacity: 2,000
Seating Capacity: 151
Web Site: www.chasetown-fc.com

GENERAL INFORMATION

Car Parking: At the ground
Coach Parking: At the ground
Nearest Railway Station: Cannock (5 miles)
Club Shop: At the ground
Opening Times: Matchdays only
Telephone Nº: (01543) 682222

GROUND INFORMATION

Away Supporters' Entrances & Sections:
No usual segregation

ADMISSION INFO (2011/2012 PRICES)

Adult Standing/Seating: £9.00
Concessionary Standing/Seating: £5.00
Under-16s Standing/Seating: £3.00
Note: Under-5s are admitted free of charge as are the Under-11s if accompanied by a paying adult
Programme Price: £2.00

DISABLED INFORMATION

Wheelchairs: Accommodated
Helpers: Admitted
Prices: Normal prices apply for the disabled and helpers
Disabled Toilets: None
Contact: (01543) 682222   (Bookings are not necessary)

Travelling Supporters' Information:
Routes: Take the A5190 to Burntwood. At the roundabout in the centre of Burntwood, turn onto the High Street (B5011), take the first exit at the next roundabout and continue heading southwards along the High Steet. Take the 3rd exit at the roundabout at the end of the road into Church Street and the ground is on the left after approximately 400 yards.

CHESTER FC

Founded: 1885
Former Names: Chester FC and Chester City FC
Nickname: 'City'
Ground: Exacta Stadium, Bumpers Lane, Chester, CH1 4LT **Ground Telephone Nº:** (01244) 371376
Pitch Size: 116 × 75 yards

Record Attendance: 5,987 (17th April 2004)
Colours: Blue and White striped shirts, Black shorts
Ticket Office: (01244) 371376
Fax Number: (01244) 390265
Ground Capacity: 5,556 **Seating Capacity:** 4,170
Web site: www.chesterfc.com

GENERAL INFORMATION

Car Parking: Ample spaces available at the ground (£1.00)
Coach Parking: Available at the ground
Nearest Railway Station: Chester (2 miles)
Nearest Bus Station: Chester (1½ miles)
Club Shop: At the ground
Opening Times: Weekdays & matchdays 10.00am–4.00pm
Telephone Nº: (01244) 371376

GROUND INFORMATION

Away Supporters' Entrances & Sections:
South Stand for covered seating and also part of the West Stand

ADMISSION INFO (2011/2012 PRICES)

Adult Standing: £10.00   **Adult Seating:** £12.00
Senior Citizen Standing: £7.00   **Seating:** £8.00
Under-18s Seating/Standing: £5.00
Under-16s Seating/Standing: £3.00   (Under-5s free)
Programme Price: £2.50

DISABLED INFORMATION

Wheelchairs: 32 spaces for wheelchairs (with 40 helpers) in the West Stand and East Stand
Helpers: One helper admitted per disabled person
Prices: Concessionary prices for the disabled. Free for helpers
Disabled Toilets: Available in West and East Stands
Contact: (01244) 371376   (Bookings are necessary)

Travelling Supporters' Information:
Routes: From the North: Take the M56, A41 or A56 into the Town Centre and then follow Queensferry (A548) signs into Sealand Road. Turn left at the traffic lights by 'Tesco' into Bumpers Lane – the ground is ½ mile at the end of the road; From the East: Take the A54 or A51 into the Town Centre (then as North); From the South: Take the A41 or A483 into Town Centre (then as North); From the West: Take the A55, A494 or A548 and follow Queensferry signs towards Birkenhead (A494) and after 1¼ miles bear left onto the A548 (then as North); From the M6/M56 (Avoiding Town Centre): Take the M56 to Junction 16 (signposted Queensferry), turn left at the roundabout onto A5117, signposted Wales. At the next roundabout turn left onto the A5480 (signposted Chester) and after approximately 3 miles take the 3rd exit from the roundabout (signposted Sealand Road Industrial Parks). Go straight across 2 sets of traffic lights into Bumpers Lane. The ground is ½ mile on the right.

CHORLEY FC

Founded: 1883
Former Names: None
Nickname: 'Magpies'
Ground: Victory Park Stadium, Duke Street, Chorley, PR7 3DU
Record Attendance: 9,679 (1931/32 season)
Pitch Size: 112 × 72 yards

Colours: Black & White striped shirts with Black shorts
Telephone Nº: (01257) 263406
Fax Number: (01257) 275662
Ground Capacity: 4,100
Seating Capacity: 900
Web site: www.chorleyfc.com

GENERAL INFORMATION

Car Parking: 80 spaces available at the ground
Coach Parking: At the ground
Nearest Railway Station: Chorley (¼ mile)
Nearest Bus Station: 15 minutes from the ground
Club Shop: At the ground
Opening Times: Matchdays only
Telephone Nº: –

GROUND INFORMATION

Away Supporters' Entrances & Sections:
Pilling Lane Stand entrances and accommodation

ADMISSION INFO (2010/2011 PRICES)

Adult Standing: £8.00
Adult Seating: £8.00
Concessionary Standing/Seating: £4.00
Under-16s Standing/Seating: £4.00
Programme Price: £2.00

DISABLED INFORMATION

Wheelchairs: Accommodated by prior arrangement
Helpers: Please contact the club for information
Prices: Please contact the club for information
Disabled Toilets: Available
Contact: (01257) 230007 (Bookings are not necessary)

Travelling Supporters' Information:
Routes: Exit the M61 at Junction 6 and follow the A6 to Chorley. Going past the Yarrow Bridge Hotel on Bolton Road, turn left at the 1st set of traffic lights into Pilling Lane. Take the 1st right into Ashby Street and the ground is the 2nd entrance on the left; Alternative Route: Exit the M6 at Junction 27 and follow signs to Chorley. Turn left at the lights and continue down the A49 for 2½ miles before turning right onto B5251. On entering Chorley, turn right into Duke Street 200 yards past The Plough.

FC UNITED OF MANCHESTER

FC United of Manchester are currently groundsharing with Bury FC.

Founded: 2005
Nickname: 'F.C.'
Ground: Gigg Lane, Bury, Lancashire BL9 9HR
Ground Capacity: 11,313 (All seats)
Pitch Size: 112 × 70 yards
Record Attendance: 6,731 (8th December 2010)

Colours: Red shirts with White shorts
Office Address: Hope Mills, 113 Pollard Street, Ancoats, Manchester M4 7JA
Telephone Nº: (0161) 273-8950
Fax Number: (0161) 273-7598
Web Site: www.fc-utd.co.uk

GENERAL INFORMATION

Car Parking: Designated car parks only
Coach Parking: By Police direction
Nearest Railway Station: Bury Interchange (1 mile)
Nearest Bus Station: Bury Interchange
Club Shop: At the ground and via the Club's web site
Opening Times: Matchdays only, before and after the game
Telephone Nº: (0161) 273-8950

GROUND INFORMATION

Away Supporters' Entrances & Sections:
Gigg Lane entrance for the West Stand

ADMISSION INFO (2011/2012 PRICES)

Adult Seating: £8.00
Senior Citizen Seating: £5.00
Under-18s Seating: £2.00
Programme Price: £2.00

DISABLED INFORMATION

Wheelchairs: Spaces for 46 wheelchairs in disabled sections (home area) and a further 8 spaces in the Away Supporters' Section
Helpers: One helper admitted per wheelchair
Prices: Wheelchair users and one helper are admitted free
Disabled Toilets: Available in disabled section
Contact: (0161) 273-8950 (Bookings are not necessary)

Travelling Supporters' Information: Routes: From the North: Exit the M66 at Junction 2, take Bury Road (A58) for ½ mile, then turn left into Heywood Street and follow this into Parkhills Road until its end, turn left into Manchester Road (A56) and then left again into Gigg Lane. From the South, East and West: Exit the M60 at Junction 17, take Bury Road (A56) for 3 miles and then turn right into Gigg Lane.

14

FRICKLEY ATHLETIC FC

Founded: 1910
Former Names: Frickley Colliery FC
Nickname: 'The Blues'
Ground: Tech5 Stadium, Westfield Lane, South Elmsall, Pontefract WF9 2EQ
Record Attendance: 6,500 (1971)
Pitch Size: 117 × 75 yards

Colours: Blue and White striped shirts, Blue shorts
Telephone Nº: (01977) 642460
Daytime Phone Nº: 07985 291074
Fax Number: (01977) 642460
Ground Capacity: 6,000
Seating Capacity: 800
Web site: www.frickleyafc.co.uk

GENERAL INFORMATION

Car Parking: 200 spaces available at the ground
Coach Parking: At the ground
Nearest Railway Station: South Elmsall (1 mile)
Nearest Bus Station: South Elmsall
Club Shop: At the ground
Opening Times: 1 hour before kick-off and during half-time
Telephone Nº: (01977) 642460

GROUND INFORMATION

Away Supporters' Entrances & Sections:
No usual segregation

ADMISSION INFO (2011/2012 PRICES)

Adult Standing/Seating: £8.00
Senior Citizen Standing/Seating: £5.00
Under-16s Standing/Seating: £3.00
Note: Under-16s are admitted free of charge when accompanied by a paying adult
Programme Price: £1.50

DISABLED INFORMATION

Wheelchairs: Accommodated in a new disabled area
Helpers: Please phone the club for information
Prices: Please phone the club for information
Disabled Toilets: Available in the Stand and at the Bar
Contact: (01977) 648365   (Bookings are not necessary)

Travelling Supporters' Information:
Routes: From the North: Follow the A1 Southbound and take the first exit after the Trusthouse Forte Travelodge and follow the road to South Kirkby then on to South Emsall. Upon entering the Town Centre, take Westfield Lane then Oxford Street. The ground is at the bottom on the right; From the South: Take the M1, M18 and A1(M) and finally the A638. Follow the road towards Wakefield then to South Emsall, then as above; From the West and East: Take the M62 to the junction with the A1 and head south to the first exit. Then as above.

HEDNESFORD TOWN FC

Founded: 1880
Former Names: Formed by the amalgamation of West Hill FC and Hill Top FC
Nickname: 'The Pitmen'
Ground: Keys Park, Keys Park Road, Hednesford, Cannock WS12 2DZ
Record Attendance: 3,169 (13th January 1997)

Colours: White shirts and shorts
Telephone Nº: (01543) 422870
Fax Number: (01543) 428180
Ground Capacity: 6,039
Seating Capacity: 1,011
Pitch Size: 110 × 70 yards
Web site: www.hednesfordfc.co.uk

GENERAL INFORMATION

Car Parking: 500 spaces available at the ground – £1.00 fee
Coach Parking: At the ground
Nearest Railway Station: Hednesford (1 mile)
Nearest Bus Station: Hednesford
Club Shop: At the ground
Opening Times: Matchdays and Weekdays 9.00am–5.00pm
Telephone Nº: (01543) 422870

GROUND INFORMATION

Away Supporters' Entrances & Sections:
No usual segregation

ADMISSION INFO (2011/2012 PRICES)

Adult Standing: £9.00
Adult Seating: £10.00
Concessionary Standing: £5.00
Concessionary Seating: £6.00
Note: A selection of family tickets are also available
Programme Price: £2.00

DISABLED INFORMATION

Wheelchairs: 8 spaces available in front of the Main Stand
Helpers: Please contact the club for details
Prices: Please contact the club for details
Disabled Toilets: 2 are available – one in the Main Building, one in the Hednesford End of the stand
Contact: (01543) 422870 (Bookings are necessary)

Travelling Supporters' Information:
Routes: Exit the M6 at Junction 11 or the M6 Toll T7 and follow signs for A460 (Rugeley). After crossing the A5 at Churchbridge Island, continue on the A460. After five traffic islands pick up signs for Hednesford Town FC/Keys Park and follow to the ground.

KENDAL TOWN FC

Founded: 1920
Former Names: Netherfield FC, Netherfield Kendal FC and Kendal FC
Nickname: 'Town'
Ground: Parkside Road, Kendal   LA9 7BL
Record Attendance: 5,184 vs Grimsby Town
Pitch Size: 119 × 76 yards

Colours: Black & White striped shirts, Black shorts
Telephone N°: (01539) 727472 or (01539) 722469
Fax Number: (01539) 727472
Ground Capacity: 3,500
Seating Capacity: 395
Web site: www.kendaltownfootballclub.co.uk

GENERAL INFORMATION

Car Parking: At the ground
Coach Parking: At the ground
Nearest Railway Station: Oxenholme (2 miles)
Nearest Bus Station: Kendal (1 mile)
Club Shop: At the ground
Opening Times: Matchdays only
Telephone N°: (01539) 727472

GROUND INFORMATION

Away Supporters' Entrances & Sections:
No usual segregation

ADMISSION INFO (2011/2012 PRICES)

Adult Standing/Seating: £8.00
Senior Citizen Standing/Seating: £4.00
Under-16s Standing/Seating: £2.00
Note: Under-16s accompanied by an adult pay £1.00
Programme Price: £1.00

DISABLED INFORMATION

Wheelchairs: Accommodated
Helpers: Admitted
Prices: Normal prices apply for the disabled and helpers
Disabled Toilets: Available in the Clubhouse
Contact: (01539) 722469   (Bookings are necessary)

Travelling Supporters' Information:
Routes: Exit the M6 at Junction 36 and follow the A590 onto the A591 and finally the A6 for Kendal. Upon entering Kendal turn right at the first set of traffic lights then left at the roundabout. Turn right opposite the 'K' Village into Parkside Road and the ground is located on the right over the brow of the hill.

MARINE FC

Founded: 1894
Former Names: None
Nickname: 'Mariners' 'Lilywhites'
Ground: Arriva Stadium, College Road, Crosby, Liverpool L23 3AS
Record Attendance: 4,000 (1949)
Pitch Size: 110 × 70 yards

Colours: White shirts with Black shorts
Telephone Nº: (0151) 924-1743
Fax Number: (0151) 924-1743
Ground Capacity: 3,000
Seating Capacity: 400
Web site: www.marinefc.com

GENERAL INFORMATION

Car Parking: 30 spaces available at the ground
Coach Parking: Available outside the ground
Nearest Railway Station: Blundellsands and Crosby (800 yards)
Nearest Bus Station: Crosby
Club Shop: At the ground
Opening Times: Matchdays only
Telephone Nº: (0151) 286-9101

GROUND INFORMATION

Away Supporters' Entrances & Sections:
Entrance at Gates 1 & 2

ADMISSION INFO (2011/2012 PRICES)

Adult Standing: £9.00
Adult Seating: £9.00
Concessionary Standing: £5.00
Concessionary Seating: £5.00
Note: Under-11s are admitted free of charge when accompanied by a paying adult
Programme Price: £2.00

DISABLED INFORMATION

Wheelchairs: Accommodated the disabled area in the Millennium Stand
Helpers: Admitted
Prices: Normal prices apply for disabled and helpers
Disabled Toilets: Yes
Contact: (0151) 924-1743   (Bookings are not necessary)

Travelling Supporters' Information:
Routes: Take the M57/M58 Motorway to the end. Follow signs into Crosby town centre and the ground is situated on College Road which is off the main Liverpool to Southport A565 road. The ground is signposted in town.

MATLOCK TOWN FC

Founded: 1885
Former Names: Hall Leys FC
Nickname: 'The Gladiators'
Ground: Reynolds Stadium, Causeway Lane, Matlock DE4 3AR
Record Attendance: 5,123 (1975)
Pitch Size: 110 × 70 yards

Colours: Royal Blue shirts and shorts
Telephone/Fax No: (01629) 583866
Ground Capacity: 5,500
Seating Capacity: 560
Web site: www.matlocktownfc.co.uk

GENERAL INFORMATION

Car Parking: Available in the Town Centre (500 yards)
Coach Parking: Available at the Bus Station (300 yards)
Nearest Railway Station: Matlock (¼ mile)
Nearest Bus Station: Matlock (¼ mile)
Club Shop: At the ground
Opening Times: Weekdays 9.00am – 4.00pm and Saturdays 9.00am to 12.00pm
Telephone No: (01629) 583866

GROUND INFORMATION

Away Supporters' Entrances & Sections:
No usual segregation

ADMISSION INFO (2011/2012 PRICES)

Adult Standing: £9.00
Adult Seating: £9.00
Senior Citizen/Junior Standing: £5.50
Senior Citizen/Junior Seating: £5.50
Note: Under-15s are admitted for £2.00 when accompanied by a paying adult
Programme Price: £1.50

DISABLED INFORMATION

Wheelchairs: Accommodated
Helpers: Admitted
Prices: Normal prices apply
Disabled Toilets: Available
Contact: (01629) 583866   (Bookings are not necessary)

Travelling Supporters' Information:
Routes: Take the A6 to Matlock and at the roundabout by the Bus Station take the A615. The ground is situated on the A615 Matlock to Alfreton road about 500 yards from the Town Centre near Firs Parade.

MICKLEOVER SPORTS FC

Founded: 1948
Former Names: Mickleover Old Boys FC
Nickname: 'Sports'
Ground: Mickleover Sports Club, Station Road, Mickleover DE3 9FB
Record Attendance: 795

Colours: Red and Black striped shirts with Black shorts
Telephone No: (01332) 512826
Ground Capacity: 1,500
Seating Capacity: 280
Pitch Size: 109 × 71 yards
Web site: www.pitchero.com/clubs/mickleoversports

GENERAL INFORMATION

Car Parking: At the ground
Coach Parking: At the ground
Nearest Railway Station: Derby (4½ miles)
Club Shop: A shop at the ground is to open during the 2010/2011 season
Opening Times: Matchdays only once the shop is open
Telephone No: (01332) 521167

GROUND INFORMATION

Away Supporters' Entrances & Sections:
No usual segregation

ADMISSION INFO (2011/2012 PRICES)

Adult Standing/Seating: £9.00
Concessionary Standing/Seating : £5.00
Under-16s Standing/Seating: £1.00
Programme Price: £1.50

DISABLED INFORMATION

Wheelchairs: Accommodated
Helpers: Admitted
Prices: Concessionary prices are charged to the disabled and helpers
Disabled Toilets: Available in the Clubhouse
Contact: (01332) 521167 (Bookings are not necessary)

Travelling Supporters' Information:
Routes: From the South: Take the A38 to Mickleover and exit at the junction with the A516 near the hospital. Take the 3rd exit at the large roundabout joining the B5020 Uttoxeter Road, passing under the A38 and heading into Mickleover. Turn right at the roundabout into Station Road and the ground is on the right hand side just before the junction with Radbourne Lane; From the A52: Exit the A52 at Kirk Langley and follow the B5020 Moor Lane southwards towards Mickleover. Upon reaching Mickleover, turn right into Station Road (still the B5020) and the Sports Club is on the left hand side of the road.

NANTWICH TOWN FC

Founded: 1884
Former Names: None
Nickname: 'Dabbers'
Ground: Weaver Stadium, Water-Lode, Kingsleyfields, Nantwich CW5 5BS
Record Attendance: 5,121 (1920/21 season)
Pitch Size: 109 × 71 yards

Colours: Green and White halved shirts, Green shorts
Telephone Nº: (01270) 621771
Fax Number: (01270) 611930
Ground Capacity: 3,500
Seating Capacity: 350
Web Site: www.nantwichtownfc.com

GENERAL INFORMATION
Car Parking: At the ground
Coach Parking: At the ground
Nearest Railway Station: Nantwich (1 mile)
Club Shop: At the ground
Opening Times: Tuesdays to Saturdays 11.00am to 1.00pm
Telephone Nº: (01270) 621771

GROUND INFORMATION
Away Supporters' Entrances & Sections:
No usual segregation

ADMISSION INFO (2011/2012 PRICES)
Adult Standing: £9.00
Adult Seating: £9.00
Concessionary Standing: £6.00
Concessionary Seating: £6.00
Under-16s Standing: £2.00
Under-16s Seating: £2.00
Programme Price: £2.00

DISABLED INFORMATION
Wheelchairs: Accommodated
Helpers: Admitted
Prices: Normal prices apply for the disabled. Free of charge for helpers
Disabled Toilets: Available
Contact: E-mail: sarah.laws@nantwichtownfc.com

Travelling Supporters' Information:
Routes: From the South: Take the A529 or A530 to Nantwich, continue northwards along the A530 Wellington Road, pass the railway station, then turn left at the roundabout into Water-Lode. Continue along Water-Lode which becomes the A534 and the ground is on the right after approximately ½ mile; From the East or West: Take the A534 to Nantwich. Follow signs for the A534 road into Water-Lode for the ground; From the North-West: Take the A51 towards Nantwich, join the A534 and follow the road to Water-Lode for the ground; From the North-East: Take the A530 into the centre of Nantwich then head westward on the A534 for Water-Lode and the ground.

NORTH FERRIBY UNITED FC

Founded: 1934
Former Names: None
Nickname: 'Villagers' or 'Green & Whites'
Ground: Rapid Solicitors Stadium, Church Road, North Ferriby, East Yorkshire   HU14 3AB
Record Attendance: 2,000   (vs Hull City in 2009)
Pitch Size: 109 × 76 yards

Colours: Green shirts with White trim, Green shorts
Telephone Nº: (01482) 634601
Fax Number: (01482) 634601
Ground Capacity: 2,500
Seating Capacity: 250
Web site: www.northferribyunited.com

GENERAL INFORMATION
Car Parking: Limited spaces at the ground
Coach Parking: At the ground
Nearest Railway Station: Ferriby (5 minutes walk)
Nearest Bus Station: Hull
Club Shop: At the ground
Opening Times: Matchdays only
Telephone Nº: (01482) 634601

GROUND INFORMATION
Away Supporters' Entrances & Sections:
No usual segregation

ADMISSION INFO (2011/2012 PRICES)
Adult Standing: £9.00
Adult Seating: £9.00
Senior Citizen/Under-16s Standing: £4.00
Senior Citizen/Under-16s Seating: £5.00
Programme Price: £2.00

DISABLED INFORMATION
Wheelchairs: Accommodated
Helpers: Admitted
Prices: Standard prices apply
Disabled Toilets: Available
Contact: (01482) 634601   (Bookings are not necessary)

Travelling Supporters' Information:
Routes: North Ferriby is approximately 8 miles to the west of Hull on the A63. Upon reaching North Ferriby (from the West), proceed through the village past the Duke of Cumberland Hotel and turn right into Church Lane. The ground is situated on the left after half a mile.

NORTHWICH VICTORIA FC

Founded: 1874
Former Names: None
Nickname: 'The Vics' 'The Greens' 'The Trickies'
Ground: Victoria Stadium, Wincham Avenue, Wincham, Northwich   CW9 6GB
Record Attendance: 3,216 (April 2006)
Pitch Size: 112 × 74 yards

Colours: Green and White hooped shirts with White shorts
Office Telephone Nº: (01606) 815208
Fax Number: (01606) 815242
Ground Capacity: 5,046
Seating Capacity: 1,180
Web site: www.northwichvics.co.uk

GENERAL INFORMATION

Car Parking: Ample parking spaces available at the ground
Coach Parking: At the ground
Nearest Railway Station: Northwich (1½ miles)
Nearest Bus Station: Northwich (2½ miles)
Club Shop: At the ground
Opening Times: Weekdays & Matchdays 10.00am–4.00pm
Telephone Nº: (01606) 815200

GROUND INFORMATION

Away Supporters' Entrances & Sections:
West Terrace

ADMISSION INFO (2011/2012 PRICES)

Adult Standing: £10.00
Adult Seating: £12.00
Senior Citizen Standing: £8.00
Senior Citizen Seating: £10.00
Under-16s Standing/Seating: £5.00
Under-12s Standing/Seating: £2.00
Programme Price: £2.00

DISABLED INFORMATION

Wheelchairs: 52 spaces are available in total
Helpers: Admitted
Prices: Normal prices for the disabled. Free for the helpers
Disabled Toilets: Yes
Contact: (01606) 815200   (Please phone to book)

Travelling Supporters' Information:
Routes: Exit the M6 at Junction 19 and take the A556 towards Northwich. After 3 miles turn right onto the A559 following signs for Warrington. Turn left after Marston opposite the Black Greyhound Inn then left into Wincham Avenue after 200 yards.
Alternative Route: Exit the M56 at Junction 10 and take the A559 to the Black Greyhound Inn then turn right. Then as above

RUSHALL OLYMPIC FC

Founded: 1893 (Re-formed in 1951)
Former Names: None
Nickname: 'The Pics'
Ground: Dales Lane, off Daw End Lane, Rushall, near Walsall WS4 1LJ
Record Attendance: 2,000

Colours: Gold and Black shirts with Black shorts
Telephone N°: (01922) 641021
Ground Capacity: 2,500
Seating Capacity: 200
Pitch Size: 109 × 75 yards
Web Site: www.rofc.co.uk

GENERAL INFORMATION
Car Parking: At the ground
Coach Parking: At the ground
Nearest Railway Station: Walsall (3¼ miles)
Club Shop: At the ground
Opening Times: Matchdays only
Telephone N°: –

GROUND INFORMATION
Away Supporters' Entrances & Sections:
No usual segregation

ADMISSION INFO (2011/2012 PRICES)
Adult Standing/Seating: £7.50
Senior Citizen/Junior Standing/Seating: £4.00
Note: Under-12s are admitted free of charge when accompanied by a paying adult
Programme Price: £2.00

DISABLED INFORMATION
Wheelchairs: Accommodated
Helpers: Admitted
Prices: Normal prices apply for the disabled and helpers
Disabled Toilets: Available
Contact: (01922) 641021 (Bookings are not necessary)

Travelling Supporters' Information:
Routes: Exit the M6 at Junction 9 and take the A454 then the A4148 towards Walsall. Turn left onto the A461 Lichfield Street at the roundabout then take the first exit at the next roundabout continuing on A461 Lichfield Road. Pass underneath the railway bridge then turn right onto the B4154 into Daw End Lane. Cross the Rushall Canal and the entrance to the ground is on the right hand side of the road.

STAFFORD RANGERS FC

Founded: 1876
Former Names: None
Nickname: 'The Boro'
Ground: Marston Road, Stafford   ST16 3BX
Record Attendance: 8,523 (4th January 1975)
Pitch Size: 112 × 71 yards

Colours: Black and White striped shirts, Black shorts
Telephone N°: (01785) 602430
Social Club N°: (01785) 602432
Fax Number: (01785) 602431
Ground Capacity: 3,030   **Seating Capacity:** 527
Web site: www.staffordrangersfc.co.uk

GENERAL INFORMATION
Supporters Club: c/o Social Club
Telephone N°: (01785) 602432
Car Parking: At the ground
Coach Parking: Astonfields Road
Nearest Railway Station: Stafford (1½ miles)
Nearest Bus Station: Stafford
Club Shop: At the ground
Opening Times: Matchdays only
Telephone N°: (01785) 602430
Police Telephone N°: (01785) 258151

GROUND INFORMATION
Away Supporters' Entrances & Sections:
Lotus End

ADMISSION INFO (2011/2012 PRICES)
Adult Standing: £9.00
Adult Seating: £11.00
Concessionary Standing: £6.00
Concessionary Seating: £8.00
Note: Children under the age of 12 are admitted free of charge when accompanying a paying adult
Programme Price: £2.00

DISABLED INFORMATION
Wheelchairs: Accommodated at Marston Road End
Helpers: Admitted
Prices: Concessionary prices for the disabled. Normal prices for helpers
Disabled Toilets: Available
Contact: (01785) 602430   (Bookings are not necessary)

Travelling Supporters' Information:
Routes: Exit the M6 at Junction 14 and take the slip road signposted 'Stone/Stafford'. Continue to traffic island and go straight across then take the 3rd exit on the right into Common Road, signposted 'Common Road/Aston Fields Industrial Estate'. Follow the road to the bridge and bear left over the bridge. The ground is on the right.

STOCKSBRIDGE PARK STEELS FC

Founded: 1986
Former Names: None
Nickname: 'Steels'
Ground: Look Local Stadium, Bracken Moor Lane, Stocksbridge, Sheffield S36 2AN
Record Attendance: 2,050 (1991)
Pitch Size: 112 × 70 yards

Colours: Yellow shirts with Royal Blue shorts
Telephone Nº: (0114) 288-8305
Fax Number: (0114) 288-8305
Ground Capacity: 3,500
Seating Capacity: 450
Web Site: www.stocksbridgeps.com

GENERAL INFORMATION
Car Parking: At the ground
Coach Parking: At the ground
Nearest Railway Station: Penistone (6 miles)
Club Shop: At the ground
Opening Times: Matchdays only
Telephone Nº: –

GROUND INFORMATION
Away Supporters' Entrances & Sections:
No usual segregation

ADMISSION INFO (2011/2012 PRICES)
Adult Standing/Seating: £7.00
Senior Citizen Standing/Seating: £4.00
Under-16s Standing/Seating: £2.00
Programme Price: £1.50

DISABLED INFORMATION
Wheelchairs: Accommodated
Helpers: Admitted
Prices: Concessionary prices are charged for the disabled and helpers
Disabled Toilets: Available
Contact: (0114) 288-8305   (Bookings are not necessary)

Travelling Supporters' Information:
Routes: From the West: Take the A628 then A616 towards Stocksbridge then turn right onto the B6088 (Manchester Road) immediately after passing Underbank Reservoir. Continue into Stocksbridge then turn right up Nanny Hill turning into Bocking Hill. Continue along this road into Bracken Moor Lane and the ground is on the left; From the South: Take the A6102 to Deepcar then turn left into the B6088 Manchester Road. Continue into Stocksbridge then turn left into Haywood Lane, right into New Road then left into Haywood Lane once again. Turn right into Bocking Hill and continue for the ground; From the East: Take the A616 towards Stocksbridge, exit onto the A6102 and head into Deepcar. Turn right at the junction into the B6088 Manchester Road then as above.

WHITBY TOWN FC

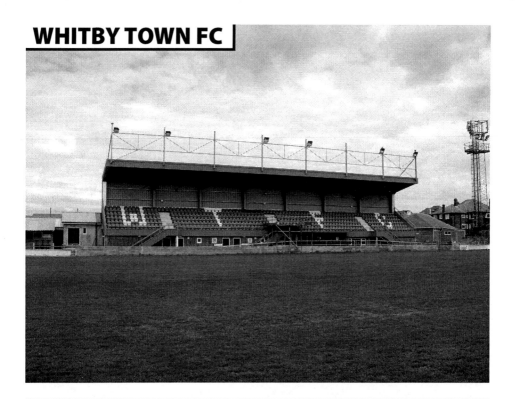

Founded: 1893
Former Names: Whitby United FC
Nickname: 'The Seasiders' or 'The Blues
Ground: Turnbull Ground, Upgang Lane, Whitby, YO21 3HZ
Record Attendance: 4,500
Pitch Size: 110 × 72 yards

Colours: Royal Blue shirts and shorts
Telephone Nº: (01947) 603193 (Clubhouse)
Daytime Phone Nº: (01947) 604847 (Office)
Fax Number: (01947) 603779
Ground Capacity: 3,200
Seating Capacity: 622
Web site: www.whitby-town.com

GENERAL INFORMATION

Car Parking: At the ground – passholders only
Coach Parking: At the ground
Nearest Railway Station: Whitby (½ mile)
Nearest Bus Station: Whitby (½ mile)
Club Shop: At the ground
Opening Times: Matchdays only
Telephone Nº: –

GROUND INFORMATION

Away Supporters' Entrances & Sections:
No usual segregation

ADMISSION INFO (2011/2012 PRICES)

Adult Standing/Seating: £8.00
Concessionary Standing/Seating: £5.00
Under-16s Standing/Seating: £2.00
Programme Price: £1.50

DISABLED INFORMATION

Wheelchairs: Accommodated in a special disabled area
Helpers: Admitted
Prices: Free for the disabled. Helpers charged normal prices
Disabled Toilets: One available
Contact: (01947) 603193 (Bookings are not necessary)

Travelling Supporters' Information:
Routes: On entering Whitby from the west on either the A169 or A171 road, take the first fork and follow signs for the "West Cliff". Turn left at the Spar shop and garage into Love Lane and continue to the junction with the A174. Turn right onto the A174 and the ground is on the left hand side after approximately 600 yards.

WORKSOP TOWN FC

Founded: 1861 (Reformed in 1893)
Former Names: None
Nickname: 'The Tigers'
Ground: Babbage Way, off Sandy Lane, Worksop, S80 1TN
Record Attendance: 2,115
Pitch Size: 120 × 74 yards

Colours: Amber and Black shirts with Black shorts
Telephone Nº: 07734 144961
Fax Number: (01909) 487934
Ground Capacity: 2,500
Seating Capacity: 1,000
Web site: www.worksoptownfc.co.uk

GENERAL INFORMATION

Car Parking: Adjacent to the ground
Coach Parking: Adjacent to the ground
Nearest Railway Station: Worksop (2 minutes walk)
Nearest Bus Station: Worksop (2 minutes walk)
Club Shop: At the ground
Opening Times: Matchdays only
Telephone Nº: None

GROUND INFORMATION

Away Supporters' Entrances & Sections:
No usual segregation

ADMISSION INFO (2011/2012 PRICES)

Adult Standing: £10.00
Adult Seating: £10.00
Child Standing: £5.00
Child Seating: £5.00
Note: Under-16s are admitted free of charge when accompanying a paying adult (maximum of 2 per adult)
Programme Price: £2.00

DISABLED INFORMATION

Wheelchairs: Accommodated
Helpers: Admitted
Prices: Normal prices apply for the disabled and helpers
Disabled Toilets: Available
Contact: 07734 144961 (Bookings are not necessary)

Travelling Supporters' Information:
Routes: Exit the M1 at Junction 31 from the north or Junction 30 from the South and follow signs for Worksop. After reaching Worksop, carry on to the bypass and, at the 3rd roundabout (next to Sainsburys), turn off following signs for Sandy Lane Industrial Estate. The ground is on the left after half a mile.

THE EVO-STIK NORTHERN PREMIER LEAGUE DIVISION ONE NORTH

Secretary Angie Firth   **Phone** (01422) 410691

Address 23 High Lane, Norton Tower, Halifax HX2 0MW

Web Site evostikleague.pitchero.com

Clubs for the 2011/2012 Season

AFC FYLDE

Founded: 1988	**Colours:** White shirts and shorts
Former Names: Formed by the amalgamation of Wesham FC and Kirkham Town FC in 1988	**Telephone Nº:** (01772) 682593
	Fax Number: (01772) 685893
Nickname: 'The Coasters'	**Ground Capacity:** 1,426
Ground: Kellamergh Park, Bryning Lane, Warton, Preston PR4 1TN	**Seating Capacity:** 282
	Pitch Size: 110 × 82 yards
Record Attendance: 1,390 (17th July 2009)	**Web Site:** www.afcfylde.co.uk

GENERAL INFORMATION

Car Parking: At the ground
Coach Parking: At the ground
Nearest Railway Station: Moss Side (2¼ miles)
Club Shop: 6 Station Road, Kirkham PR4 2AS
Opening Times: Matchdays only
Telephone Nº: (01772) 682593 (Phone orders accepted)

GROUND INFORMATION

Away Supporters' Entrances & Sections:
No usual segregation

ADMISSION INFO (2011/2012 PRICES)

Adult Standing: £7.00
Adult Seating: £7.00
Concessionary Standing: £5.00
Concessionary Seating: £5.00
Under-16s Standing: £3.00
Under-16s Seating: £3.00
Note: Under-12s are admitted free of charge when accompanying a paying adult
Programme Price: £2.00

DISABLED INFORMATION

Wheelchairs: Accommodated
Helpers: Admitted
Prices: Normal prices apply for the disabled. Helpers pay concessionary prices
Disabled Toilets: None
Contact: (01772) 682593 (Bookings are not necessary)

Travelling Supporters' Information:
Routes: Exit the M55 at Junction 3 and take the A585 (signposted Fleetwood/Kirkham). At the roundabout outside of Kirkham, take the 2nd exit continuing on the A585, go straight on at the next roundabout, then at the roundabout junction with the A583, take the 2nd exit onto the B5259 Ribby Road. Follow this road into Wrea Green, then turn left by the Green itself into Bryning Lane. Continue for about 1 mile and the ground is situated on the left of the road.

BAMBER BRIDGE FC

Founded: 1952
Former Names: None
Nickname: 'The Brig'
Ground: Irongate Ground, Brownedge Road, Irongate, Bamber Bridge, Preston   PR5 6UX
Record Attendance: 3,250 (28th March 1992)
Pitch Size: 110 × 74 yards

Colours: White shirts with Black shorts
Telephone Nº: (01772) 909690
Fax Number: (01772) 909691
Ground Capacity: 2,600
Seating Capacity: 250
Web site: www.bamberbridgefc.co.uk

GENERAL INFORMATION
Car Parking: At the ground
Coach Parking: At the ground
Nearest Railway Station: Bamber Bridge (1¼ miles)
Nearest Bus Station: Preston
Club Shop: At the ground
Opening Times: One hour before kick-off on matchdays
Telephone Nº: –

GROUND INFORMATION
Away Supporters' Entrances & Sections:
No usual segregation

ADMISSION INFO (2011/2012 PRICES)
Adult Standing: £8.00
Adult Seating: £8.00
Senior Citizen/Student Standing: £4.00
Senior Citizen/Student Seating: £4.00
Note: Under-16s are admitted free of charge when accompanying a paying adult
Programme Price: £1.00

DISABLED INFORMATION
Wheelchairs: Accommodated
Helpers: Please phone the club for information
Prices: Please phone the club for information
Disabled Toilets: Available
Contact: (01772) 909690   (Bookings are necessary)

Travelling Supporters' Information:
Routes: Exit the M6 at Junction 29 and follow Preston signs to the major roundabout onto London Way. Take the 3rd exit at the next roundabout signposted Bamber Bridge. Take the 1st right and at the end of the road after 100 yards turn left into the ground.

CAMMELL LAIRD FC

Founded: 1889
Former Names: Grange FC, Cammell Laird Institute FC and Cammell Laird Sports Club
Nickname: 'Lairds'
Ground: Kirklands, St. Peters Road, Rock Ferry, Birkenhead CH42 1PY
Record Attendance: 1,700 (1990/91 season)

Colours: Royal Blue shirts and shorts
Telephone N°: (0151) 645-3121 (Social Club)
Fax Number: (0151) 644-7354
Ground Capacity: 2,000
Seating Capacity: 150
Pitch Size: 110 × 71 yards
Web Site: www.pitchero.com/clubs/cammelllaird

GENERAL INFORMATION
Car Parking: At the ground
Coach Parking: At the ground
Nearest Railway Station: Rock Ferry (½ mile)
Club Shop: At the ground
Opening Times: Matchdays only
Telephone N°: –

GROUND INFORMATION
Away Supporters' Entrances & Sections:
No usual segregation

ADMISSION INFO (2011/2012 PRICES)
Adult Standing: £6.00
Adult Seating: £6.00
Senior Citizen/Junior Standing: £3.00
Senior Citizen/Junior Seating: £3.00
Programme Price: £2.00

DISABLED INFORMATION
Wheelchairs: Accommodated
Helpers: Admitted
Prices: Normal prices apply for the disabled and helpers
Disabled Toilets: None
Contact: (0151) 645-3121 (Bookings are not necessary)

Travelling Supporters' Information:
Routes: The ground is situated in the Rock Ferry area in the south of Birkenhead, just off the B5136 New Chester Road. Leave the New Chester Road at Rock Ferry, turning into Rock Lane East then turn immediately right into St. Peters Road. The ground is on the right hand side of the road after a short distance.

CLITHEROE FC

Founded: 1877
Former Names: Clitheroe Central FC
Nickname: 'The Blues'
Ground: Shawbridge, Off Pendle Road, Clitheroe, BB7 1LZ
Record Attendance: 2,050 (1995/96 season)

Colours: Blue shirts and shorts
Telephone N°: (01200) 423344
Fax Number: (01200) 444487
Ground Capacity: 2,400
Seating Capacity: 250
Web Site: www.clitheroefc.co.uk (Unofficial site)

GENERAL INFORMATION

Car Parking: At the ground
Coach Parking: At the ground
Nearest Railway Station: Clitheroe (½ mile)
Club Shop: In the Clubhouse at the ground
Opening Times: Matchdays only
Telephone N°: –

GROUND INFORMATION

Away Supporters' Entrances & Sections:
No usual segregation

ADMISSION INFO (2011/2012 PRICES)

Adult Standing: £7.00
Adult Seating: £7.00
Senior Citizen Standing: £4.00
Senior Citizen Seating: £4.00
Under-18s Standing/Seating: £2.00
Note: Under-14s are admitted free of charge when accompanying a paying adult
Programme Price: £1.50

DISABLED INFORMATION

Wheelchairs: Accommodated
Helpers: Admitted
Prices: Normal prices apply for the disabled and helpers
Disabled Toilets: Available
Contact: (01200) 444487 (Bookings are not necessary)

Travelling Supporters' Information:
Routes: Exit the M6 at Junction 31 and take the A59 towards Blackburn. At the end of the short section of dual-carriageway, bear left at the Swallow Hotel and continue along the A59 to Clitheroe. At the junction with the A671 just to the south of Clitheroe, continue along the A59 then take the next turning signposted for Clitheroe onto Pendle Road. Take the first exit at the mini-roundabout and you'll need to find a parking space once you see the postbox on your left. The ground itself is further along on the right behind the Bridge pub and the turnstile is up the narrow lane to the right of the pub.

CURZON ASHTON FC

Founded: 1963
Former Names: None
Nickname: 'The Blues'
Ground: Tameside Stadium, Richmond Street, Ashton-under-Lyne OL7 9HG
Record Attendance: 1,826
Pitch Size: 114 × 72 yards

Colours: Royal Blue shirts and shorts
Telephone Nº: (0161) 330-6033
Fax Number: (0161) 339-8802
Ground Capacity: 5,000
Seating Capacity: 504
Web Site: www.curzon-ashton.co.uk

GENERAL INFORMATION
Car Parking: At the ground
Coach Parking: At the ground
Nearest Railway Station: Ashton-under-Lyne (1 mile)
Club Shop: At the ground
Opening Times: Matchdays only
Telephone Nº: (0161) 330-6033

GROUND INFORMATION
Away Supporters' Entrances & Sections:
No usual segregation

ADMISSION INFO (2011/2012 PRICES)
Adult Standing: £7.00
Adult Seating: £7.00
Senior Citizen/Junior Standing: £2.50
Senior Citizen/Junior Seating: £2.50
Programme Price: £1.50

DISABLED INFORMATION
Wheelchairs: Accommodated
Helpers: Admitted
Prices: Normal prices apply for the disabled and helpers
Disabled Toilets: Available
Contact: (0161) 330-6033 (Bookings are not necessary)

Travelling Supporters' Information:
Routes: Exit the M60 at Junction 23 and take the A6140 signposted for Ashton. Continue along the A6140 to the set of traffic lights with a Cinema on the right then turn left. Cross over a bridge and go straight across the mini-roundabout before turning left into the ground. NOTE: Diversions may be in force during the 2010/2011 season due to bridge replacement work.

DURHAM CITY FC

Founded: 1918 (Re-formed 1949)
Former Names: None
Nickname: 'City'
Ground: The Durham UTS Arena, New Ferens Park, Belmont Industrial Estate, Durham   DH1 1GG
Record Attendance: 2,750 (2001/02 season)

Colours: Yellow and Blue halved shirts, Blue shorts
Telephone Nº: (0191) 386-9616
Ground Capacity: 2,700
Seating Capacity: 270
Pitch Size: 109 × 77 yards
Web Site: www.durhamcityafc.com

GENERAL INFORMATION
Car Parking: At the ground
Coach Parking: At the ground
Nearest Railway Station: Durham (2¾ miles)
Club Shop: None
Opening Times: –
Telephone Nº: –

GROUND INFORMATION
Away Supporters' Entrances & Sections:
No usual segregation

ADMISSION INFO (2011/2012 PRICES)
Adult Standing: £8.00
Adult Seating: £8.00
Senior Citizen Standing: £5.00
Senior Citizen Seating: £5.00
Under-15s Standing/Seating: £2.00 (Free of charge when accompanying a paying adult)
Programme Price: £2.00

DISABLED INFORMATION
Wheelchairs: Accommodated
Helpers: Admitted
Prices: Normal prices apply for the disabled and helpers
Disabled Toilets: Available
Contact: (0191) 386-9616   (Bookings are not necessary)

Travelling Supporters' Information:
Routes: Exit the A1(M) at Junction 62 and follow the A690 signs for Durham City. Turn off at the first slip road into Broomside Lane then turn left again into the Industrial Estate. The ground is on the left after approximately 150 yards.

FARSLEY AFC

Founded: 1908 (Original club)
Former Names: Farsley Celtic FC
Nickname: 'Villagers'
Ground: Throstle Nest, Newlands, Farsley, Leeds, LS28 5BE
Record Attendance: 2,462 (2006)
Pitch Size: 110 × 67 yards

Colours: Blue shirts and shorts
Telephone Nº: (0113) 255-7292
Fax Number: (0113) 255-1519
Ground Capacity: 4,000
Seating Capacity: 500
Web site: www.farsleyafc.co.uk

GENERAL INFORMATION

Car Parking: Available at the ground
Coach Parking: Available at the ground
Nearest Railway Station: New Pudsey (1 mile)
Nearest Bus Station: Pudsey (1 mile)
Club Shop: At the ground
Opening Times: Weekday evenings 6.00pm – 11.00pm and weekends noon until 11.00pm
Telephone Nº: (0113) 255-7292

GROUND INFORMATION

Away Supporters' Entrances & Sections:
No usual segregation

ADMISSION INFO (2011/2012 PRICES)

Adult Standing/Seating: £9.00
Senior Citizen/Student Standing/Seating: £4.00
Child Standing/Seating: £1.00
Programme Price: £2.00

DISABLED INFORMATION

Wheelchairs: Accommodated
Helpers: Please phone the club for information
Prices: Please phone the club for information
Disabled Toilets: Available
Contact: (0113) 255-7292 (Bookings are necessary)

Travelling Supporters' Information:
Routes: From the North: Take the A1 to Wetherby then the A58 to Leeds. After about 8 miles take the 3rd exit at the roundabout onto the A6120 Ring Road. Follow signs for Bradford for approximately 12 miles and at the 7th roundabout take the B6157 signposted Stanningley. Continue for ½ mile passing the Police Station on the left then turn left down New Street (at the Tradex Warehouse). Turn right into Newlands and the ground is situated at the end of the road next to a new housing development.

GARFORTH TOWN FC

Founded: 1964
Former Names: Miners Arms FC, Garforth Miners FC
Nickname: 'The Miners'
Ground: Genix Healthcare Stadium, Cedar Ridge, Garforth, Leeds LS25 2PF
Record Attendance: 1,385

Colours: Yellow shirts with Green trim, Blue shorts
Telephone Nº: (0113) 287-7145
Ground Capacity: 3,000
Seating Capacity: 260
Pitch Size: 109 × 70 yards
Web Site: www.garforthtown.com

GENERAL INFORMATION
Car Parking: At the ground
Coach Parking: At the ground
Nearest Railway Station: East Garforth (1¼ miles)
Club Shop: At the ground
Opening Times: Matchdays only
Telephone Nº: (0113) 287-7145

GROUND INFORMATION
Away Supporters' Entrances & Sections:
No usual segregation

ADMISSION INFO (2011/2012 PRICES)
Adult Standing: £7.00
Adult Seating: £7.00
Senior Citizen/Junior Standing: £3.00
Senior Citizen/Junior Seating: £3.00
Programme Price: £2.00

DISABLED INFORMATION
Wheelchairs: Accommodated
Helpers: Admitted
Prices: Normal prices apply for the disabled and helpers
Disabled Toilets: Available
Contact: (0113) 287-7145 (Bookings are not necessary)

Travelling Supporters' Information:
Routes: Exit the M1 at Junction 47 and take the A642 (Aberford Road) towards Garforth. Take the first turning on the left into Cedar Ridge and the ground is situated at the end of the road on the right.

HARROGATE RAILWAY ATHLETIC FC

Founded: 1935
Former Names: None
Nickname: 'The Rail'
Ground: Station View, Starbeck, Harrogate, HG2 7JA
Record Attendance: 3,500 (2002/03 season)
Pitch Size: 109 × 76 yards

Colours: Red shirts with Green shorts
Telephone Nº: (01423) 883104
Ground Capacity: 3,500
Seating Capacity: 800
Web Site:
www.pitchero.com/clubs/harrogaterailwayathletic

GENERAL INFORMATION

Car Parking: At the ground
Coach Parking: As directed by the club
Nearest Railway Station: Starbeck (adjacent)
Club Shop: At the ground
Opening Times: Matchdays only
Telephone Nº: –

GROUND INFORMATION

Away Supporters' Entrances & Sections:
No usual segregation

ADMISSION INFO (2011/2012 PRICES)

Adult Standing: £7.00
Adult Seating: £7.00
Concessionary Standing: £4.00
Concessionary Seating: £4.00
Under-14s Standing/Seating: Free of charge
Programme Price: £1.50

DISABLED INFORMATION

Wheelchairs: Accommodated
Helpers: Admitted
Prices: Free of charge for the disabled and helpers by prior arrangement
Disabled Toilets: None
Contact: (01423) 883104 (Bookings are not necessary)

Travelling Supporters' Information:
Routes: Exit the A1 at Junction 47 and take the A59 towards Knaresborough and Harrogate. Follow the A59 through Knaresborough and continue into the Starbeck area of Harrogate where the A59 is the High Street. Cross over the railway line then turn right along Station View and the ground is on the left after approximately 400 yards.

LANCASTER CITY FC

Founded: 1905
Former Names: Lancaster Athletic FC,
Lancaster Town FC and City of Lancaster AFC
Nickname: 'Dolly Blues'
Ground: Giant Axe, West Road, Lancaster LA1 5PE
Record Attendance: 7,500 (1936)
Pitch Size: 110 × 78 yards

Colours: Blue shirts with White shorts
Telephone Nº: (01524) 382238
Fax Number: (01524) 382238
Ground Capacity: 3,153
Seating Capacity: 500
Web site: www.lancastercityfc.com

GENERAL INFORMATION

Car Parking: At the ground
Coach Parking: At the ground
Nearest Railway Station: Lancaster (2 minutes walk)
Nearest Bus Station: Lancaster (5 minutes walk)
Club Shop: At the ground
Opening Times: Matchdays only
Telephone Nº: None

GROUND INFORMATION

Away Supporters' Entrances & Sections:
No usual segregation

ADMISSION INFO (2011/2012 PRICES)

Adult Standing/Seating: £7.00
Concessionary/Student Standing/Seating: £5.00
Under-16s Standing/Seating: £1.00
Note: Under-12s admitted free of charge with a paying adult
Programme Price: £1.50

DISABLED INFORMATION

Wheelchairs: Accommodated
Helpers: Admitted
Prices: Normal prices apply
Disabled Toilets: Yes
Contact: (01524) 382238

Travelling Supporters' Information:
Routes: From the South: Exit the M6 at Junction 33 and follow Railway Station signs into the City. Turn left at the traffic lights after Waterstones Bookshop then take the second right passing the Railway Station on the right. Follow the road down the hill and the ground is 1st right; From the North: Exit the M6 at Junction 34 and bear left onto the A683. Go into the one-way system in the City and pass the Police Station. At the next traffic lights by the Revolution pub, follow the road back into the centre, then as from the South, following Railway Station signs.

MOSSLEY AFC

Founded: 1903
Former Names: None
Nickname: 'Lilywhites'
Ground: Seel Park, Market Street, Mossley, Ashton-under-Lyne   OL5 OES
Record Attendance: 7,000 (1950)

Colours: White shirts and shorts
Telephone Nº: (01457) 832369
Fax Number: (01457) 832369
Ground Capacity: 4,500   **Seating Capacity:** 250
Pitch Size: 110 × 71 yards
Web site: www.mossleyweb.com

GENERAL INFORMATION
Car Parking: At the ground
Coach Parking: At the ground
Nearest Railway Station: Mossley (½ mile)
Nearest Bus Station: Mossley (¼ mile)
Club Shop: At the ground
Opening Times: Matchdays only
Telephone Nº: (01457) 836104

GROUND INFORMATION
Away Supporters' Entrances & Sections:
No usual segregation

ADMISSION INFO (2011/2012 PRICES)
Adult Standing/Seating: £8.00
Senior Citizen Standing/Seating: £5.00
Child Standing/Seating: £1.00
Note: Children are admitted free when with a paying adult
Programme Price: £1.00

DISABLED INFORMATION
Wheelchairs: Accommodated
Helpers: Admitted
Prices: Normal prices apply for the disabled and helpers
Disabled Toilets: Available in the Clubhouse
Contact: (01457) 836104   (Bookings are necessary)

Travelling Supporters' Information:
Routes: Exit the M60 at Junction 23 and follow the A635. Take the 3rd exit at the first roundabout then the 3rd exit at the next roundabout by Asda. Take the 3rd exit again at the next roundabout (signposted Mossley A670) and turn right at the junction onto Mossley Road. Continue through the traffic lights and after approximately 2½ miles follow the road downhill into Mossley Town Centre. Pass the supermarket on the left and turn right before the next set of traffic lights. Continue up the hill bearing left into Market Street and the ground is on the left after 200 yards.

OSSETT ALBION FC

Founded: 1944
Former Names: None
Nickname: 'Albion'
Ground: The Warehouse Systems Stadium, Queen's Terrace, Dimple Wells Road, Ossett   WF5 8JT
Record Attendance: 1,280 (1986)

Colours: Old Gold shirts with Black shorts
Telephone Nº: (01924) 273746
Ground Capacity: 3,000
Seating Capacity: 250
Pitch Size: 114 × 77 yards
Web Site: www.pitchero.com/clubs/ossettalbion

GENERAL INFORMATION

Car Parking: At the ground
Coach Parking: At the ground
Nearest Railway Station: Dewsbury (3 miles)
Club Shop: At the ground
Opening Times: Matchdays only
Telephone Nº: –

GROUND INFORMATION

Away Supporters' Entrances & Sections:
No usual segregation

ADMISSION INFO (2011/2012 PRICES)

Adult Standing: £7.00
Adult Seating: £7.00
Senior Citizen/Student Standing: £4.00
Senior Citizen/Student Seating: £4.00
Under-16s Standing/Seating: £1.00
Programme Price: £1.50

DISABLED INFORMATION

Wheelchairs: Accommodated
Helpers: Admitted
Prices: Normal prices apply for the disabled and helpers
Disabled Toilets: Available in the Social Club (100 yards)
Contact: (01924) 273749   (Bookings are not necessary)

Travelling Supporters' Information:
Routes: Exit the M1 at Junction 40 and take the A638 westwards. After 200 yards take the slip road onto the B6129 Wakefield Road and, after approximately ½ mile, turn left into Dale Street (still B6129). Take the 4th turn on the left into the B6128 Prospect Road then turn left at the roundabout into Station Road. Turn right into Southdale Road, right again at the T-junction then immediately left into Dimple Wells Road. The entrance to the ground is straight ahead through the gap between the houses.

OSSETT TOWN FC

Founded: 1936
Former Names: None
Nickname: 'Town'
Ground: Ingfield Ground, Prospect Road, Ossett, WF5 9HA
Record Attendance: 2,600 (vs Manchester United)
Pitch Size: 110 × 72 yards

Colours: Red shirts and shorts
Telephone Nº: (01924) 280028 (Office) or (01924) 272960 (Clubhouse)
Fax Number: (01924) 280090
Ground Capacity: 4,000
Seating Capacity: 360
Web site: www.ossetttown.co.uk

GENERAL INFORMATION
Car Parking: Available behind the Bus Station (opposite)
Coach Parking: Behind the Bus Station
Nearest Railway Station: Wakefield Central (3 miles)
Nearest Bus Station: Ossett (opposite the ground)
Club Shop: At the ground
Opening Times: Matchdays only
Telephone Nº: (01924) 272960

GROUND INFORMATION
Away Supporters' Entrances & Sections:
No usual segregation

ADMISSION INFO (2011/2012 PRICES)
Adult Standing: £7.00
Adult Seating: £7.00
Senior Citizen/Concessionary Standing: £3.00
Senior Citizen/Concessionary Seating: £3.00
Child Standing/Seating: £1.00
Programme Price: £1.00

DISABLED INFORMATION
Wheelchairs: Accommodated
Helpers: Admitted
Prices: Normal prices apply
Disabled Toilets: Available in the Club room
Contact: (01924) 272960 (Bookings are not necessary)

Travelling Supporters' Information:
Routes: Exit the M1 at Junction 40 and take the A639 following signs for Ossett. Take the 1st left onto Wakefield Road then the 6th turning on the left into Dale Street (B6120). Turn left at the traffic lights and the ground is opposite the bus station.

PRESCOT CABLES FC

Founded: 1886
Former Names: Prescot Athletic FC, Prescot Town FC and Prescot FC
Nickname: 'Tigers'
Ground: Valerie Park, Eaton Street, Prescot, L34 6HD
Record Attendance: 8,122 (1932)
Pitch Size: 110 × 70 yards

Colours: Amber shirts with Black shorts
Telephone Nº: (0151) 430-0507
Contact Telephone Nº: (0151) 426-6440
Fax Number: (0151) 430-0507
Ground Capacity: 4,400
Seating Capacity: 500
Web site: www.prescotcables.co.uk

GENERAL INFORMATION
Car Parking: At the ground
Coach Parking: At the ground
Nearest Railway Station: Prescot (½ mile)
Nearest Bus Station: Prescot (¼ mile)
Club Shop: At the ground
Opening Times: Matchdays only
Telephone Nº: (0151) 430-0507

GROUND INFORMATION
Away Supporters' Entrances & Sections:
No usual segregation

ADMISSION INFO (2011/2012 PRICES)
Adult Standing: £7.00
Adult Seating: £7.00
Senior Citizen/Junior Standing: £4.00
Senior Citizen/Junior Seating: £4.00
Under-16s Standing/Seating: £2.00
Famoly Ticket: £10.00 (1 adult + 2 children)
Programme Price: £1.50

DISABLED INFORMATION
Wheelchairs: Accommodated
Helpers: Admitted
Prices: Normal prices apply
Disabled Toilets: Available
Contact: (0151) 426-6440 (Bookings are not necessary)

Travelling Supporters' Information:
Routes: Exit the M62 at Junction 7 and take the A57 signposted Rainhill & Prescot. After about 2½ miles, take the 3rd exit at the roundabout. Turn right after ½ mile at the Hope & Anchor pub into Hope Street and the ground is at the end of the road.

RADCLIFFE BOROUGH FC

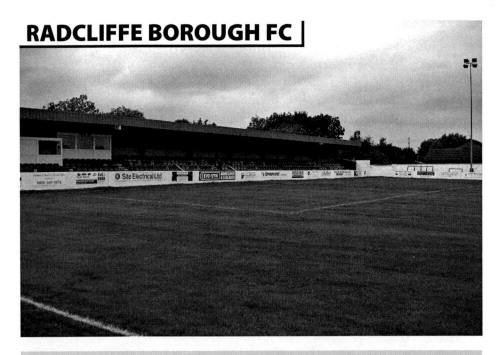

Founded: 1949
Former Names: None
Nickname: 'Boro'
Ground: Stainton Park Stadium, Pilkington Road, Radcliffe, Manchester M26 3PE
Record Attendance: 1,468 (1982)
Pitch Size: 112 × 72 yards

Colours: Blue and Black striped shirts, Black shorts
Telephone No: (0161) 724-8346 (Office)
Fax Number: (0161) 723-3178
Ground Capacity: 3,500
Seating Capacity: 350
Web site: www.pitchero.com/clubs/radcliffeborough

GENERAL INFORMATION
Car Parking: At the ground
Coach Parking: At the ground
Nearest Railway Station: Radcliffe (2 miles)
Nearest Bus Station: Radcliffe (opposite Asda – 3 miles)
Club Shop: At the ground
Opening Times: Matchdays only
Telephone No: (0161) 724-8346

GROUND INFORMATION
Away Supporters' Entrances & Sections:
No usual segregation

ADMISSION INFO (2011/2012 PRICES)
Adult Standing: £7.00
Adult Seating: £7.00
Senior Citizen Standing: £5.00
Senior Citizen Seating: £5.00
Under 16s Standing/Seating: £2.00
Note: Under-14s are admitted free of charge when accompanied by a paying adult
Programme Price: £1.50

DISABLED INFORMATION
Wheelchairs: 4 spaces available under cover
Helpers: Admitted
Prices: Please phone the club for information
Disabled Toilets: Available
Contact: (0161) 724-8346 (Bookings are not necessary)

Travelling Supporters' Information:
Routes: Exit the M60 at Junction 17 and follow signs for Whitefield and Bury. Take the A665 to Radcliffe via the bypass to Bolton Road. Turn right into Unsworth Street opposite the Turf Hotel. After about ½ mile turn left into Colshaw Close East for the ground.

SALFORD CITY FC

Founded: 1940
Former Names: Salford FC, Salford Amateurs FC plus a number of other early names
Nickname: 'The Ammies'
Ground: Moor Lane, Kersal, Salford, Manchester, M7 3PZ
Record Attendance: 3,000 (1980)

Colours: Tangerine shirts with Black shorts
Telephone Nº: (0161) 792-6287
Ground Capacity: 8,000
Seating Capacity: 260
Pitch Size: 110 × 70 yards
Web Site: www.salfordcityfc.co.uk

GENERAL INFORMATION
Car Parking: Street parking only
Coach Parking: At the ground
Nearest Railway Station: Clifton (2½ miles)
Club Shop: At the ground
Opening Times: Matchdays only
Telephone Nº: –

GROUND INFORMATION
Away Supporters' Entrances & Sections:
No usual segregation

ADMISSION INFO (2011/2012 PRICES)
Adult Standing: £7.00
Adult Seating: £7.00
Senior Citizen/Junior Standing: £3.00
Senior Citizen/Junior Seating: £3.00
Note: Under-11s are admitted free of charge
Programme Price: £1.50

DISABLED INFORMATION
Wheelchairs: Accommodated
Helpers: Admitted
Prices: Concessionary prices are charged for the disabled and helpers
Disabled Toilets: None
Contact: (0161) 792-6287 (Bookings are not necessary)

Travelling Supporters' Information:
Routes: Exit the M60 at Junction 17 and take the A56 Bury New Road towards Prestwich. Continue along, passing the A6044 (Hilton Lane) road then turn right along Moor Lane heading towards Kersal Moor and the Golf Course. The ground is on the left hand side of the road after a few hundred yards.

SKELMERSDALE UNITED FC

Founded: 1882
Former Names: None
Nickname: 'Skem'
Ground: West Lancashire College Stadium, Stormy Corner, Selby Place, Stanley Industrial Estate, Skelmersdale WN8 8EF
Record Attendance: 7,000 (1967)

Colours: Royal Blue shirts and shorts
Telephone No: (01695) 722123
Fax Number: (01695) 722123
Ground Capacity: 2,300
Seating Capacity: 240
Pitch Size: 110 × 70 yards
Web: www.pitchero.com/clubs/skelmersdaleunited

GENERAL INFORMATION

Car Parking: At the ground
Coach Parking: At the ground
Nearest Railway Station: Parbold (4 miles)
Club Shop: At the ground
Opening Times: Matchdays only
Telephone No: (01695) 722123

GROUND INFORMATION

Away Supporters' Entrances & Sections:
No usual segregation

ADMISSION INFO (2011/2012 PRICES)

Adult Standing/Seating: £8.00
Senior Citizen Standing/Seating: £4.00
Child Standing/Seating: £2.00
Note: Children are admitted free when with a paying adult
Programme Price: £1.50

DISABLED INFORMATION

Wheelchairs: Accommodated
Helpers: Admitted
Prices: Normal prices apply for the disabled. Helpers are charged concessionary prices
Disabled Toilets: Available
Contact: (01695) 722123 (Bookings are not necessary)

Travelling Supporters' Information:
Routes: Exit the M58 at Junction 4 and head into Skelmersdale. Continue straight on at the roundabout into Glenburn Road then turn left at the next roundabout into Neverstitch Road, following signs for Stanley Industrial Estate. Turn right at the next roundabout into Staveley Road then left into Statham Road. The ground is on the left in Selby Place after 500 yards.

TRAFFORD FC

Founded: 1990
Former Names: North Trafford FC
Nickname: 'The North'
Ground: Shawe View, Pennybridge Lane, Flixton, Manchester M41 5DL
Record Attendance: 803 (1997/98 season)

Colours: White shirts and shorts
Telephone No: (0161) 747-1727
Ground Capacity: 2,500
Seating Capacity: 284
Pitch Size: 111 × 75 yards
Web Site: www.traffordfc.co.uk

GENERAL INFORMATION
Car Parking: At the ground
Coach Parking: At the ground
Nearest Railway Station: Chassen Road (¼ mile)
Club Shop: None
Opening Times: –
Telephone No: –

GROUND INFORMATION
Away Supporters' Entrances & Sections:
No usual segregation

ADMISSION INFO (2011/2012 PRICES)
Adult Standing/Seating: £7.00
Senior Citizen/Junior Standing/Seating: £3.50
Note: Under-12s are admitted free of charge when accompanying a paying adult
Programme Price: £1.50

DISABLED INFORMATION
Wheelchairs: Accommodated
Helpers: Admitted
Prices: Normal prices apply for the disabled and helpers
Disabled Toilets: Available in the Clubhouse
Contact: (0161) 747-1727 (Bookings are not necessary)

Travelling Supporters' Information:
Routes: Exit the M60 at Junction 8 and take the A6144 (M) towards Lymm, Partington and Carrington. At the second set of traffic lights, turn right onto the B5158 towards Flixton. Continue along the B5158 crossing the railway bridge by Flixton Railway Station then turn right at the next set of traffic lights, passing "The Bird I'th Hand" public house. Take an immediate right turn into Pennybridge Lane and the ground is on the left after 300 yards.

WAKEFIELD FC

Wakefield FC are groundsharing with Ossett Town FC during the 2011/2012 season.

Founded: 1903
Former Names: Emley FC and Wakefield-Emley FC
Nickname: 'The Bears'
Ground: Ingfield Ground, Prospect Road, Ossett, WF5 9HA
Record Attendance: 1,378 (at Wakefield)

Colours: Royal Blue shirts and shorts
Contact Telephone N°: 07921 156561
Ground Capacity: 4,000
Seating Capacity: 360
Pitch Size: 110 × 72 yards
Web Site: www.wakefieldfc.com

GENERAL INFORMATION

Car Parking: Available behind the Bus Station (opposite)
Coach Parking: Behind the Bus Station
Nearest Railway Station: Wakefield Central (3 miles)
Nearest Bus Station: Ossett (opposite the ground)
Club Shop: At the ground (in the Bar)
Opening Times: Matchdays only
Telephone N°: –

GROUND INFORMATION

Away Supporters' Entrances & Sections:
No usual segregation

ADMISSION INFO (2011/2012 PRICES)

Adult Standing/Seating: £7.00
Concessionary Standing/Seating: 3.50
Student Standing/Seating: £3.50
Child Standing/Seating: £1.00
Programme Price: £1.50

DISABLED INFORMATION

Wheelchairs: Accommodated
Helpers: Admitted
Prices: Normal prices apply
Disabled Toilets: Available in the Club room
Contact: 07921 156561 (Bookings are not necessary)

Travelling Supporters' Information:
Routes: Exit the M1 at Junction 40 and take the A639 following signs for Ossett. Take the 1st left onto Wakefield Road then the 6th turning on the left into Dale Street (B6120). Turn left at the traffic lights and the ground is opposite the bus station.

WARRINGTON TOWN FC |

Founded: 1948
Former Names: Stockton Heath FC
Nickname: 'The Town'
Ground: Cantilever Park, Loushers Lane, Latchford, Warrington WA4 2RS
Record Attendance: Not known
Pitch Size: 112 × 72 yards

Colours: Yellow and Blue shirts with Blue shorts
Telephone N°: (01925) 653044
Fax Number: (01925) 653044
Ground Capacity: 1,600
Seating Capacity: 350
Web Site: www.warringtontownfc.co.uk

GENERAL INFORMATION
Car Parking: Street parking only
Coach Parking: Street parking only
Nearest Railway Station: Warrington Central (2 miles)
Club Shop: None
Opening Times: –
Telephone N°: –

GROUND INFORMATION
Away Supporters' Entrances & Sections:
No usual segregation

ADMISSION INFO (2011/2012 PRICES)
Adult Standing: £8.00
Adult Seating: £8.00
Senior Citizen Standing: £5.00
Senior Citizen Seating: £5.00
Under-16s Standing/Seating: £2.00
Note: Under-12s are admitted free of charge

DISABLED INFORMATION
Wheelchairs: Accommodated
Helpers: Admitted
Prices: Normal prices apply for the disabled and helpers
Disabled Toilets: None
Contact: (01925) 653044   (Bookings are not necessary)

Travelling Supporters' Information:
Routes: Exit the M6 at Junction 20 and take the A50 (signposted Warrington/Lymm). Stay on this road (Knutsford Road) and cross the Manchester Ship Canal before turning left into the B5157 Station Road. At the end of the road, turn left into Wash Lane and the ground is immediately ahead.

WITTON ALBION FC

Founded: 1887
Former Names: None
Nickname: 'Albion'
Ground: Wincham Park, Chapel Street, Wincham, Northwich CW9 6DA
Record Attendance: 3,940 (vs Kidderminster Harriers)
Pitch Size: 110 × 74 yards

Colours: Red and White striped shirts, Blue shorts
Telephone Nº: (01606) 43008
Fax Number: (01606) 43008
Ground Capacity: 4,386
Seating Capacity: 646
Web site: www.wittonalbion.com

GENERAL INFORMATION

Car Parking: 1,200 spaces available at the ground
Coach Parking: At the ground
Nearest Railway Station: Northwich
Nearest Bus Station: Northwich
Club Shop: At the ground
Opening Times: Matchdays and Thursday evenings only
Telephone Nº: (01606) 43008

GROUND INFORMATION

Away Supporters' Entrances & Sections:
Lostock End

ADMISSION INFO (2011/2012 PRICES)

Adult Standing/Seating: £8.50
Senior Citizen Standing/Seating: £5.50
Students & Under-16s Standing/Seating: £4.00
Under-14s Standing/Seating: Free of charge
Programme Price: £1.50

DISABLED INFORMATION

Wheelchairs: Accommodated in the Grandstand
Helpers: Admitted
Prices: Standard prices apply
Disabled Toilets: Available
Contact: (01606) 43008   (Bookings are recommended)

Travelling Supporters' Information:
Routes: Exit the M6 at Junction 19 and take the A556 towards Northwich. After 3 miles turn right onto the A559 following signs for Warrington. Turn left opposite the Black Greyhound Inn and the ground is on the left.
Alternative Route: Exit the M56 at Junction 10 and take the A559. Turn right at the Black Greyhound in for the ground.

WOODLEY SPORTS FC

Founded: 1970
Former Names: None
Nickname: 'The Steelmen'
Ground: The Neil Rourke Stadium, Lambeth Grove, Woodley, Stockport   SK6 1QX
Record Attendance: 1,500

Colours: Red and Blue striped shirts with Blue shorts
Telephone Nº: (0161) 406-6896
Ground Capacity: 2,300
Seating Capacity: 300
Pitch Size: 116 × 71 yards
Web Site: www.pitchero.com/clubs/woodleysports

GENERAL INFORMATION
Car Parking: At the ground
Coach Parking: At the ground
Nearest Railway Station: Woodley (½ mile walk)
Club Shop: None
Opening Times: –
Telephone Nº: –

GROUND INFORMATION
Away Supporters' Entrances & Sections:
No usual segregation

ADMISSION INFO (2011/2012 PRICES)
Adult Standing: £7.00
Adult Seating: £7.00
Senior Citizen/Junior Standing: £4.00
Senior Citizen/Junior Seating: £4.00
Programme Price: –

DISABLED INFORMATION
Wheelchairs: Accommodated
Helpers: Admitted
Prices: Normal prices apply for the disabled and helpers
Disabled Toilets: Available in the Social Club
Contact: (0161) 406-6896   (Bookings are not necessary)

Travelling Supporters' Information:
Routes: Exit the M60 at Junction 25 and take the A560 towards Woodley. Pass Bredbury Station on the right and the junction with the A627 (George Lane) then take an immediate left into Mill Lane. Continue over the railway line and take the 5th turn on the right into Wood Grove. At the crossroad, turn left along Lambeth Grove and the ground is on the left after 150 yards.

THE EVO-STIK
NORTHERN PREMIER LEAGUE
DIVISION ONE SOUTH

Secretary Angie Firth   **Phone** (01422) 410691

Address 23 High Lane, Norton Tower, Halifax HX2 0MW

Web Site evostikleague.pitchero.com

Clubs for the 2011/2012 Season

BELPER TOWN FC

Founded: 1883
Former Names: None
Nickname: 'The Nailers'
Ground: Christchurch Meadow, Bridge Street, Belper DE56 1BA
Record Attendance: 3,200 (1955)
Pitch Size: 109 × 75 yards

Colours: Yellow shirts with Black shorts
Telephone Nº: (01773) 825549
Fax Number: (01773) 825549
Ground Capacity: 2,600
Seating Capacity: 500
Web Site: www.belpertownfc.co.uk

GENERAL INFORMATION

Car Parking: A car park is adjacent to the ground
Coach Parking: Outside the ground
Nearest Railway Station: Belper (¼ mile)
Club Shop: At the ground
Opening Times: Matchdays only
Telephone Nº: –

GROUND INFORMATION

Away Supporters' Entrances & Sections:
No usual segregation

ADMISSION INFO (2011/2012 PRICES)

Adult Standing: £7.00
Adult Seating: £7.00
Senior Citizen/Under-16s Standing: £3.50
Senior Citizen/Under-16s Seating: £3.50
Note: Under-14s are admitted for £1.00 when accompanied by a paying adult.
Programme Price: £1.50

DISABLED INFORMATION

Wheelchairs: Accommodated
Helpers: Admitted
Prices: Normal prices apply for the disabled and helpers
Disabled Toilets: Available
Contact: (01773) 825549 (Bookings are not necessary)

Travelling Supporters' Information:
Routes: Exit the M1 at Junction 28 and take the A38 towards Derby. Turn off onto the A610 near Ripley and head towards Ambergate. Turn left onto the A6 at the junction by the Hurt Arms Hotel and follow into Belper. The ground is located directly off the A6 and is accessed by turning right down the lane by the side of the Church just after the first set of traffic lights.

BRIGG TOWN FC

Founded: 1864
Former Names: None
Nickname: 'The Zebras'
Ground: The Hawthorns, Hawthorn Avenue, Brigg DN20 8PG   (SatNav: DN20 8DT)
Record Attendance: 2,000 (1952)
Pitch Size: 110 × 75 yards

Colours: Black & White striped shirts with Black shorts
Telephone Nº: (01652) 651605
Fax Number: (01652) 651605
Ground Capacity: 2,000
Seating Capacity: 650
Web Site: www.briggtownfc.info

GENERAL INFORMATION
Car Parking: At the ground and street parking
Coach Parking: At the ground
Nearest Railway Station: Brigg (¾ mile)
Club Shop: At the ground
Opening Times: Matchdays only
Telephone Nº: (01652) 651605

GROUND INFORMATION
Away Supporters' Entrances & Sections:
No usual segregation

ADMISSION INFO (2011/2012 PRICES)
Adult Standing: £7.00
Adult Seating: £7.00
Senior Citizen/Junior Standing: £5.00
Senior Citizen/Junior Seating: £5.00
Programme Price: £1.50

DISABLED INFORMATION
Wheelchairs: Accommodated
Helpers: Admitted
Prices: Normal prices apply for the disabled. Helpers are charged concessionary prices
Disabled Toilets: None
Contact: (01652) 651605   (Bookings are necessary)

Travelling Supporters' Information:
Routes: Exit the M180 at Junction 5 and take the A18 towards Brigg. Pass through Wrawby and, upon reaching Brigg, turn right opposite the cemetery following the signpost for "Brigg Town FC" and follow the road around to the ground.

CARLTON TOWN FC

Founded: 1904	**Colours:** Yellow and Blue striped shirts, Blue shorts
Former Names: Sneinton FC	**Telephone N°:** (0115) 940-3192 (Office)
Nickname: 'Town'	**Ground Capacity:** 1,500
Ground: Bill Stokeld Stadium, Stoke Lane, Gedling,	**Seating Capacity:** 164
Nottingham NG4 2QP	**Pitch Size:** 109 × 70 yards
Record Attendance: 1,000	**Web Site:** www.carltontownfc.co.uk

GENERAL INFORMATION

Car Parking: At the ground
Coach Parking: At the ground
Nearest Railway Station: Netherfield (¾ mile)
Club Shop: At the ground
Opening Times: Matchdays only
Telephone N°: –

GROUND INFORMATION

Away Supporters' Entrances & Sections:
No usual segregation

ADMISSION INFO (2011/2012 PRICES)

Adult Standing: £7.00
Adult Seating: £7.00
Senior Citizen Standing/Seating: £5.00
Child Standing/Seating: £3.00
Programme Price: £1.50

DISABLED INFORMATION

Wheelchairs: Accommodated
Helpers: Admitted
Prices: Normal prices apply for the disabled and helpers
Disabled Toilets: Available
Contact: (0115) 940-3192 (Bookings are not necessary)

Travelling Supporters' Information:
Routes: The ground is located in Gedling on the eastern outskirts of Nottingham. Take the A612 Gedling bypass from the east or the west to the Gedling area, then turn into Stoke Lane at the traffic lights next to the Severn Trent Works. The ground is clearly visible from this junction and the entrance to the ground is immediately on the right.

COALVILLE TOWN FC

Founded: 1926
Former Names: Ravenstone Miners Athletic FC
Nickname: 'The Ravens'
Ground: Owen Street Sports Ground, Owen Street, Coalville   LE67 3DA
Record Attendance: 1,800 (2nd April 2011)
Pitch Size: 115 × 72 yards

Colours: Black & White striped shirts, White shorts
Telephone N°: (01530) 833365
Fax Number: (01530) 833365
Ground Capacity: 2,000
Seating Capacity: 240
Web Site: www.coalvilletownfc.co.uk

GENERAL INFORMATION
Car Parking: At the ground
Coach Parking: At the ground
Nearest Railway Station: Loughborough (8½ miles)
Club Shop: At the ground
Opening Times: Matchdays only 1.00pm to 4.00pm
Telephone N°: (01530) 833365

GROUND INFORMATION
Away Supporters' Entrances & Sections:
No usual segregation

ADMISSION INFO (2010/2011 PRICES)
Adult Standing: £7.00
Adult Seating: £7.00
Senior Citizen/Junior Standing: £5.00
Senior Citizen/Junior Seating: £5.00
Note: Under-5s are admitted free of charge
Programme Price: £1.00

DISABLED INFORMATION
Wheelchairs: Accommodated
Helpers: Admitted
Prices: Normal prices apply for the disabled and helpers
Disabled Toilets: Available in the clubhouse
Contact: (01530) 833365   (Bookings are not necessary)

Travelling Supporters' Information:
Routes: Take the Ashby exit from the A42 and follow the A511 to Coalville. After approximately 3 miles, take the second exit at the first roundabout then take the 3rd exit at the next roundabout into Coalville town centre. Pass through the traffic lights and over a mini-roundabout and then, after approximately 200 yards, turn right into Owen Street. The ground is at the top of the street on the left-hand side.

GOOLE AFC

Founded: 1912
Former Names: Goole Shipyards FC & Goole Town FC
Nickname: 'The Vikings'
Ground: Victoria Pleasure Grounds, Marcus Street, Goole   DN14 6WW
Record Attendance: 976 (1999)
Pitch Size: 111 × 71 yards

Colours: Red shirts and shorts
Telephone N°: (01405) 762794 or 07970 626954
Fax Number: (01430) 449222
Ground Capacity: 3,000
Seating Capacity: 250
Web Site: www.pitchero.com/clubs/gooleafc

GENERAL INFORMATION
Car Parking: At the ground and street parking
Coach Parking: At the ground
Nearest Railway Station: Goole (½ mile)
Club Shop: At the ground
Opening Times: Matchdays only
Telephone N°: –

GROUND INFORMATION
Away Supporters' Entrances & Sections:
No usual segregation

ADMISSION INFO (2011/2012 PRICES)
Adult Standing/Seating: £7.00
Senior Citizen Standing/Seating: £5.00
Junior Standing/Seating: £3.00
Programme Price: £1.50

DISABLED INFORMATION
Wheelchairs: Accommodated
Helpers: Admitted
Prices: Normal prices apply for the disabled and helpers
Disabled Toilets: None
Contact: (01405) 762794   (Bookings are not necessary)

Travelling Supporters' Information:
Routes: Exit the M62 at Junction 36 and follow signs for Goole Town Centre. Turn right at the second set of traffic lights into Boothferry Road then right again after 300 yards into Carter Street. The ground is directly ahead at the end of the road.

GRANTHAM TOWN FC

Founded: 1874
Former Names: None
Nickname: 'Gingerbreads'
Ground: South Kesteven Sports Stadium, Trent Road, Grantham, Lincolnshire NG31 7XQ
Record Attendance: 3,695 (vs Southport)
Pitch Size: 109 × 71 yards

Colours: White shirts with Black shorts
Telephone Nº: (01476) 402224
Fax Number: (01476) 419392
Ground Capacity: 2,100
Seating Capacity: 650
Web site: www.granthamtownfc.com

GENERAL INFORMATION

Car Parking: At the ground
Coach Parking: At the ground
Nearest Railway Station: Grantham
Nearest Bus Station: Grantham
Club Shop: At the ground
Opening Times: Matchdays only
Telephone Nº: (01476) 402224

GROUND INFORMATION

Away Supporters' Entrances & Sections:
Accommodation on the North Terrace

ADMISSION INFO (2011/2012 PRICES)

Adult Standing: £8.00
Adult Seating: £8.00
Concessionary Standing: £6.00
Concessionary Seating: £6.00
Under-16s Standing/Seating: Free of charge
Programme Price: £2.00

DISABLED INFORMATION

Wheelchairs: Accommodated
Helpers: Admitted
Prices: Free for the disabled. Helpers pay normal prices
Disabled Toilets: Yes
Contact: (01476) 562011   (Bookings are necessary)

Travelling Supporters' Information:
Routes: Take the A52 from Nottingham and upon entering Grantham, turn 1st right into Barrowby Gate. Turn right at the end then immediate left into Trent Road for the ground. Alternatively, take the A1 to the A607 Melton turn-off and follow signs for the Industrial Estate then turn left into Trent Road. The Ground is signposted 'Sports Complex' from all directions.

HUCKNALL TOWN FC

Founded: 1946	**Colours:** Yellow shirts with Black shorts
Former Names: Hucknall Colliery Welfare FC	**Telephone N°:** (0115) 930-206
Nickname: 'The Town'	**Fax Number:** (0115) 963-0716
Ground: Watnall Road, Hucknall, Nottinghamshire,	**Ground Capacity:** 3,012
NG15 6EY	**Seating Capacity:** 500
Record Attendance: 1,836 (9th April 2005)	**Web site:** www.hucknalltownfc.com
Pitch Size: 120 × 75 yards	

GENERAL INFORMATION
Car Parking: Available at the ground
Coach Parking: At the ground
Nearest Railway Station: Hucknall (1 mile)
Nearest Bus Station: Broadmarsh, Nottingham (change for Hucknall)
Club Shop: At the ground
Opening Times: Matchdays or by appointment only
Telephone N°: (0115) 963-0206

GROUND INFORMATION
Away Supporters' Entrances & Sections:
No usual segregation

ADMISSION INFO (2011/2012 PRICES)
Adult Standing: £8.00
Adult Seating: £8.00
Child Standing: £2.00   (Junior Members £1.00)
Child Seating: £2.00   (Junior Members £1.00)
Senior Citizen Standing: £5.00
Senior Citizen Seating: £5.00
Programme Price: £2.00

DISABLED INFORMATION
Wheelchairs: Accommodated
Helpers: Admitted
Prices: Concessionary prices are charged
Disabled Toilets: One available
Contact: (0115) 963-0206   (Bookings are not necessary)

Travelling Supporters' Information:
Routes: Exit the M1 at Junction 27 and take the A608 towards Hucknall. Turn right onto the A611 to Hucknall then take the Hucknall bypass. At the second roundabout join Watnall Road (B6009) and the ground is 100 yards on the right.

ILKESTON FC

Founded: 1945 (Re-formed 2010)
Former Names: Ilkeston Town FC
Nickname: 'Robins'
Ground: New Manor Ground, Awsworth Road, Ilkeston, Derbyshire   DE7 8JF
Record Attendance: 2,538
Pitch Size: 113 × 74 yards

Colours: Red shirts with White sleeves, Red shorts
Telephone Nº: (0115) 944-4428
Fax Number: (0115) 944-4428
Ground Capacity: 3,029
Seating Capacity: 550
Web site: www.ilkestonfc.co.uk

GENERAL INFORMATION
Car Parking: At the ground
Coach Parking: At the ground
Nearest Railway Station: Derby (9 miles)
Nearest Bus Station: Ilkeston
Club Shop: At the ground
Opening Times: Matchdays only
Telephone Nº: –

GROUND INFORMATION
Away Supporters' Entrances & Sections:
No usual segregation, but can be used if necessary

ADMISSION INFO (2010/2011 PRICES)
Adult Standing: £7.00
Adult Seating: £7.00
Senior Citizen/Under-16s Standing: £4.00
Senior Citizen/Under-16s Seating: £4.00
Note: Under-16s are admitted for £1.00 when accompanied by a paying adult
Programme Price: £2.00

DISABLED INFORMATION
Wheelchairs: Accommodated
Helpers: Admitted
Prices: Please phone the club for further information
Disabled Toilets: Available
Contact: (0115) 944-4428   (Bookings are not necessary)

Travelling Supporters' Information:
Routes: Exit the M1 at Junction 26 and take the A610 westwards for 2-3 miles. At the roundabout, turn left to Awsworth then at the next traffic island join the Awsworth Bypass following signs for Ilkeston A6096. After ½ mile turn right into Awsworth Road (signposted Cotmanhay) and the ground is ½ mile on the left.

KIDSGROVE ATHLETIC FC

Founded: 1952
Former Names: None
Nickname: 'The Grove'
Ground: The Seddon Stadium, Hollinwood Close, Kidsgrove ST7 1DQ
Record Attendance: 1,903 (1998)
Pitch Size: 109 × 76 yards

Colours: Blue shirts and shorts
Telephone Nº: (01782) 782412 (Office)
Fax Number: (01782) 782412
Ground Capacity: 2,500
Seating Capacity: 1,000
Web Site: www.pitchero.com/clubs/kidsgroveathleticfc

GENERAL INFORMATION

Car Parking: At the ground
Coach Parking: At the ground
Nearest Railway Station: Kidsgrove (¾ mile)
Club Shop: At the ground
Opening Times: Matchdays only
Telephone Nº: –

GROUND INFORMATION

Away Supporters' Entrances & Sections:
No usual segregation

ADMISSION INFO (2011/2012 PRICES)

Adult Standing: £7.00
Adult Seating: £7.00
Senior Citizen/Junior Standing: £4.00
Senior Citizen/Junior Seating: £4.00
Programme Price: £1.50

DISABLED INFORMATION

Wheelchairs: Accommodated
Helpers: Admitted
Prices: Normal prices apply for the disabled and helpers
Disabled Toilets: None
Contact: (01872) 782412 (Bookings are not necessary)

Travelling Supporters' Information:
Routes: Exit the M6 at Junction 16 and take the A500 towards Stoke. Take the first exit at the roundabout and head into Kidsgrove on the A34. Turn right at the traffic lights by the Caldwell Tavern public house then turn right again at the next set of traffic lights (by the Co-operative) into Cedar Avenue. Take the second turning on the right (opposite Second Avenue) into Lower Ash Road then the 3rd left into Hollinwood Road. The entrance to the ground is on the left.

LEEK TOWN FC

Founded: 1946
Former Names: Abbey Green Rovers FC and Leek Lowe Hamil FC
Nickname: 'The Blues'
Ground: Harrison Park, Macclesfield Road, Leek, Staffordshire   ST13 8LD
Record Attendance: 5,312 (1973/74)

Pitch Size: 111 × 71 yards
Colours: Blue shirts and shorts
Telephone Nº: (01538) 399278
Fax Number: (01538) 399278
Ground Capacity: 3,000
Seating Capacity: 640
Web site: www.pitchero.com/clubs/leektown

GENERAL INFORMATION

Car Parking: 80 spaces available at the ground
Coach Parking: At the ground
Nearest Railway Station: Stoke or Macclesfield (both are 13 miles)
Nearest Bus Station: Leek
Club Shop: At the ground
Opening Times: Matchdays only
Telephone Nº: (01538) 399278
Postal Sales: Yes

GROUND INFORMATION

Away Supporters' Entrances & Sections:
Grace Street entrances for the Grace Street Paddock

ADMISSION INFO (2011/2012 PRICES)

Adult Standing/Seating: £7.00
Child Standing/Seating: £4.00
Note: Under-11s are admitted for £1.00 if accompanied by a paying adult
Programme Price: £1.20

DISABLED INFORMATION

Wheelchairs: 5 spaces available for home fans, 4 for away fans
Helpers: Admitted
Prices: Normal prices apply
Disabled Toilets: Two available
Contact: (01538) 399278   (Bookings are not necessary)

Travelling Supporters' Information:
Routes: From the North: Exit the M6 at Junction 19 to Macclesfield then follow the A523 to Buxton Road; From the South: Exit the M6 at Junction 15 to the City Centre then follow A53 Leek Road. The ground is situated ½ mile outside Leek on the Macclesfield side of the A523 Macclesfield to Buxton road.

LINCOLN UNITED FC

Founded: 1938
Former Names: Lincoln Amateurs FC
Nickname: 'United'
Ground: Ashby Avenue, Hartsholme, Lincoln, LN6 0DY
Record Attendance: 1,200 (vs Crook Town)
Pitch Size: 110 × 72 yards

Colours: White shirts with Red shorts
Telephone N°: (01522) 696400
Social Club Number: (01522) 690674
Ground Capacity: 2,000
Seating Capacity: 400
Web site: www.pitchero.com/clubs/lincolnunited

GENERAL INFORMATION
Car Parking: At the ground
Coach Parking: At the ground
Nearest Railway Station: Lincoln Central (3 miles)
Club Shop: At the ground
Opening Times: Matchdays only
Telephone N°: (01522) 696400
Postal Sales: Yes

GROUND INFORMATION
Away Supporters' Entrances & Sections:
No usual segregation

ADMISSION INFO (2011/2012 PRICES)
Adult Standing: £6.00
Adult Seating: £6.00
Child Standing: £3.00
Child Seating: £3.00
Programme Price: £2.00

DISABLED INFORMATION
Wheelchairs: Accommodated
Helpers: Admitted
Prices: Normal prices apply
Disabled Toilets: Available
Contact: (01522) 696400   (Bookings are not necessary)

Travelling Supporters' Information:
Routes: Take the A46 Ring Road to the Birchwood exit (Skellingthorpe Road). After about 1 mile, turn right into Ashby Avenue and the ground is situated on the right after 200 yards.

LOUGHBOROUGH DYNAMO FC

Founded: 1955
Former Names: None
Nickname: 'Dynamo'
Ground: Nanpantan Sports Ground, Watermead Lane, Nanpantan Road, Loughborough   LE11 3YE
Record Attendance: Not known

Colours: Gold shirts with Black shorts
Telephone/Fax N°: (01509) 237148 (Office)
Ground Capacity: 1,500
Seating Capacity: 250
Pitch Size: 109 × 70 yards
Web Site: www.loughboroughdynamofc.co.uk

GENERAL INFORMATION

Car Parking: At the ground
Coach Parking: At the ground
Nearest Railway Station: Loughborough (2½ miles)
Club Shop: None
Opening Times: –
Telephone N°: –

GROUND INFORMATION

Away Supporters' Entrances & Sections:
No usual segregation

ADMISSION INFO (2011/2012 PRICES)

Adult Standing/Seating: £7.00
Senior Citizen Standing/Seating: £4.00
Under-16s Standing/Seating: £1.00
Note: Under-5s are admitted free of charge
Programme Price: £1.50

DISABLED INFORMATION

Wheelchairs: Accommodated
Helpers: Admitted
Prices: Normal prices apply for the disabled. Helpers are admitted free of charge
Disabled Toilets: Available
Contact: (01509) 237148   (Bookings are not necessary)

Travelling Supporters' Information:
Routes: Exit the M1 at Junction 23 and take the A512 into Loughborough. Turn right at the first set of traffic lights along Snells Nook Lane and head into Nanpanton. Turn left into Nanpanton Road at the first crossroads next to the Priory Public House, take the first turning on the right after ¾ mile into Watermead Lane and the ground is at the end of the lane.

MARKET DRAYTON TOWN FC

Founded: 1946
Former Names: Little Drayton Rangers FC
Nickname: 'The Moes'
Ground: Greenfields Sports Ground, Greenfield Lane, Market Drayton   TF9 3SL
Record Attendance: 340 (vs Telford)
Pitch Size: 109 × 71 yards

Colours: Red shirts and shorts
Telephone Nº: (01630) 655088 (Office)
Fax Number: (01630) 658859
Ground Capacity: 1,000
Seating Capacity: 250
Web Site: www.marketdraytontownfc.co.uk

GENERAL INFORMATION
Car Parking: At the ground
Coach Parking: At the ground
Nearest Railway Station: Prees (11 miles)
Club Shop: In the Social Club at the ground
Opening Times: Matchdays only
Telephone Nº: –

GROUND INFORMATION
Away Supporters' Entrances & Sections:
No usual segregation

ADMISSION INFO (2011/2012 PRICES)
Adult Standing: £7.00
Adult Seating: £7.00
Senior Citizen/Junior Standing: £4.00
Senior Citizen/Junior Seating: £4.00
Programme Price: £1.50

DISABLED INFORMATION
Wheelchairs: Accommodated
Helpers: Admitted
Prices: Concessionary prices are charged for the disabled and helpers
Disabled Toilets: Available in the Clubhouse
Contact: (01630) 655088 (Bookings are not necessary)

Travelling Supporters' Information:
Routes: Exit the M6 at Junction 15 and take the A5182 towards Market Drayton. Turn left onto the A53 and continue towards Market Drayton. Upon reaching the northern outskirts of Market Drayton, turn left onto the A529 then take the 2nd turning on the right into Greenfields Lane. The ground is on the right after ¼ mile.

NEWCASTLE TOWN FC

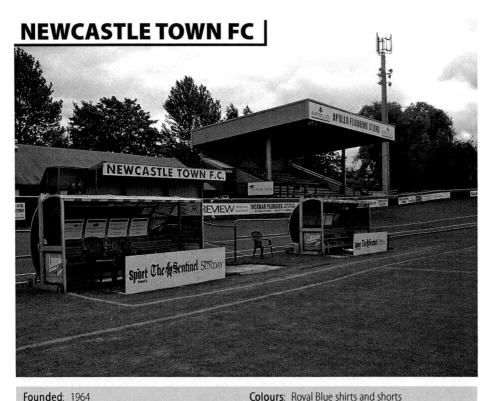

Founded: 1964
Former Names: Formed when Parkway Hanley FC and Clayton Park FC merged in 1986
Nickname: 'Castle'
Ground: Lyme Valley Stadium, Buckmaster Avenue, Clayton, Newcastle-under-Lyme   ST5 3BX
Record Attendance: 3,948 (1996)

Colours: Royal Blue shirts and shorts
Telephone Nº: (01782) 662350
Fax Number: (01782) 662350
Ground Capacity: 4,000
Seating Capacity: 300
Pitch Size: 111 × 74 yards
Web Site: www.newcastletown.co.uk

GENERAL INFORMATION

Car Parking: At the ground
Coach Parking: At the ground
Nearest Railway Station: Stoke-on-Trent (3 miles)
Club Shop: At the ground
Opening Times: Matchdays only
Telephone Nº: (01782) 662350

GROUND INFORMATION

Away Supporters' Entrances & Sections:
No usual segregation

ADMISSION INFO (2011/2012 PRICES)

Adult Standing/Seating: £6.00
Concessionary Standing/Seating: £3.00
Note: Under-16s are admitted free of charge when accompanied by a paying adult
Programme Price: £1.50

DISABLED INFORMATION

Wheelchairs: Accommodated
Helpers: Admitted
Prices: Concessionary prices are charged for the disabled and helpers
Disabled Toilets: Available
Contact: 07792 292846   (Bookings are not necessary)

Travelling Supporters' Information:
Routes: Exit the M6 at Junction 15 and take the A519 towards Newcastle-under-Lyme. Turn right at the second roundabout along Stafford Avenue then take the first left into Tittensor Road and entrance to the stadium is on the right hand side just after passing the junction with Lilleshall Road.

NEW MILLS FC

Founded: 1886
Former Names: None
Nickname: 'The Millers'
Ground: Church Lane, New Mills   SK22 4NP
Record Attendance: 4,000 (9th September 1922)
Pitch Size: 112 × 71 yards

Colours: Amber shirts and shorts
Telephone Nº: (01663) 747435
Fax Number: (01663) 747435
Ground Capacity: 1,600
Seating Capacity: 200
Web Site: www.newmillsafc.co.uk

GENERAL INFORMATION

Car Parking: At the ground
Coach Parking: At the ground
Nearest Railway Station: New Mills Newtown or New Mills Central (both approximately ½ mile)
Nearest Bus Station: Outside the ground on Church Road
Club Shop: None, but merchandise is available from behind the bar in the clubhouse and items can be purchased online through the club's web site.
Opening Times: –
Telephone Nº: (01663) 747435

GROUND INFORMATION

Away Supporters' Entrances & Sections:
No usual segregation

ADMISSION INFO (2010/2011 PRICES)

Adult Standing: £6.50
Adult Seating: £6.50
Senior Citizen/Junior Standing: £3.50
Senior Citizen/Junior Seating: £3.50
Programme Price: £1.50

DISABLED INFORMATION

Wheelchairs: Accommodated
Helpers: Admitted
Prices: Normal prices apply for the disabled and helpers
Disabled Toilets: Available
Contact: (01663) 747435   (Bookings are not necessary)

Travelling Supporters' Information:
Routes: Take the A6 to New Mills and turn right (heading from the south) or left (from the north) onto the A6015 Albion Road heading into the town centre. Pass New Mills Newtown station and continue straight through the lights past the The Queens Arms, up the hill for ½ mile and the ground is on the left at the pedestrian crossing. The car park is behind the ground.

QUORN FC

Founded: 1924
Former Names: Quorn Methodists FC
Nickname: None
Ground: Farley Way Stadium, Farley Way, Quorn, LE12 8RB
Record Attendance: 2,550 (a pre-season friendly vs Leicester City on 9th July 2008)

Colours: Red shirts and shorts
Telephone Nº: (01509) 620232
Fax Number: (01509) 620232
Ground Capacity: 2,550
Seating Capacity: 350
Pitch Size: 110 × 70 yards
Web Site: www.quornfc.com

GENERAL INFORMATION

Car Parking: At the ground
Coach Parking: At the ground
Nearest Railway Station: Barron-on-Soar (2½ miles)
Club Shop: None at present
Opening Times: –
Telephone Nº: –

GROUND INFORMATION

Away Supporters' Entrances & Sections:
No usual segregation

ADMISSION INFO (2011/2012 PRICES)

Adult Standing: £7.00
Adult Seating: £7.00
Senior Citizen/Junior Standing: £4.00
Senior Citizen/Junior Seating: £4.00
Note: Under-14s are admitted free of charge when accompanied by a paying adult
Programme Price: £1.50

DISABLED INFORMATION

Wheelchairs: Accommodated
Helpers: Admitted
Prices: Normal prices for the disabled. Helpers are admitted free of charge
Disabled Toilets: Available
Contact: (01509) 620232 (Bookings are not necessary)

Travelling Supporters' Information:
Routes: Exit the M1 at Junction 24 and take the A6 to Loughborough. Follow the A6 through Loughborough Town Centre following signs for Leicester and, after leaving the town, go straight on at the roundabout, heading for Quorn. At the first set of traffic lights, turn left into Farley Way and the entrance to the ground is immediately on the left.

RAINWORTH MINERS WELFARE FC

Founded: 1922
Former Names: None
Nickname: 'The Wrens'
Ground: Welfare Ground, Kirklington Road,
Rainworth, Mansfield   NG21 0JY
Record Attendance: 5,071
Pitch Size: 110 × 70 yards

Colours: White shirts and shorts
Telephone N°: (01623) 792495
Fax Number: (01623) 796183
Ground Capacity: 2,148
Seating Capacity: 210
Web site: www.pitchero.com/clubs/rainworthmwfc

GENERAL INFORMATION
Car Parking: At the ground
Coach Parking: At the ground
Nearest Railway Station: Mansfield Town (4¼ miles)
Club Shop: At the ground
Opening Times: Matchdays only
Telephone N°: 07740 576958

GROUND INFORMATION
Away Supporters' Entrances & Sections:
No usual segregation

ADMISSION INFO (2011/2012 PRICES)
Adult Standing: £6.00
Adult Seating: £6.00
Senior Citizen/Junior Standing: £3.00
Senior Citizen/Junior Seating: £3.00
Programme Price: £1.50

DISABLED INFORMATION
Wheelchairs: Accommodated
Helpers: Admitted
Prices: Normal prices apply for the disabled and helpers
Disabled Toilets: Available
Contact: (01623) 792495   (Bookings are not necessary)

Travelling Supporters' Information:
Routes: Take the A617 (Newark) road from Mansfield and turn off onto the B6020 at Rainworth. Continue into Rainworth along this road and turn left by the Robin Hood Public House into Kirklington Road (the old A617) when the B6020 bends to the right. The ground is then located on the left after The Potters Club.

ROMULUS FC

Romulus FC are currently groundsharing with Sutton Coldfield FC

Founded: 1979
Former Names: None
Nickname: 'The Roms'
Ground: Central Ground, Coles Lane, Sutton Coldfield, B72 1NL
Record Attendance: 407 (vs Chasetown in 2008)

Colours: Red and White shirts with Red shorts
Telephone Nº: (0121) 354-2997 (Matchdays only)
Ground Capacity: 4,500
Seating Capacity: 200
Pitch Size: 109 × 71 yards
Web Site: www.pitchero.com/clubs/romulus

GENERAL INFORMATION

Car Parking: At the ground
Coach Parking: At the ground
Nearest Railway Station: Sutton Coldfield (¾ mile)
Club Shop: None
Opening Times: –
Telephone Nº: –

GROUND INFORMATION

Away Supporters' Entrances & Sections:
No usual segregation

ADMISSION INFO (2011/2012 PRICES)

Adult Standing: £7.00
Adult Seating: £7.00
Senior Citizen/Junior Standing: £4.00
Senior Citizen/Junior Seating: £4.00
Programme Price: £1.50

DISABLED INFORMATION

Wheelchairs: Accommodated
Helpers: Admitted
Prices: Normal prices apply for the disabled and helpers
Disabled Toilets: Available
Contact: (0121) 354-2997 (Bookings are not necessary)

Travelling Supporters' Information:
Routes: Exit the M42 at Junction 9 and take the A4097 Minworth road. At Minworth roundabout, follow signs for Walmley Village and turn right at the T-junction onto the B4148 Walmley Road. Take the 3rd turning on the left into Wylde Green Road, pass over the canal and the railway bridge then turn right into East View Road which becomes Coles Road as the road bends around. The entrance to the ground is on the right between a gap in the houses.

SHEFFIELD FC

Founded: 1857 (World's Oldest Football Club)
Former Names: None
Nickname: 'Club'
Ground: The BT Local Business Stadium, Sheffield Road, Dronfield, Sheffield S18 2GD
Record Attendance: 2,000 (1976/77 season)
Pitch Size: 111 × 71 yards

Colours: Red shirts with Black shorts
Telephone Nº: (01246) 292622 (Office)
Telephone Nº: (01246) 292633
Ground Capacity: 2,089
Seating Capacity: 250
Web Site: www.sheffieldfc.com

GENERAL INFORMATION
Car Parking: At the ground
Coach Parking: At the ground
Nearest Railway Station: Dronfield (approximately 1 mile)
Club Shop: At the ground
Opening Times: Weekdays and Matchdays
Telephone Nº: (01246) 292622

GROUND INFORMATION
Away Supporters' Entrances & Sections:
No usual segregation

ADMISSION INFO (2011/2012 PRICES)
Adult Standing: £6.00
Adult Seating: £6.00
Senior Citizen/Junior Standing: £3.00
Senior Citizen/Junior Seating: £3.00
Programme Price: £1.50

DISABLED INFORMATION
Wheelchairs: Accommodated
Helpers: Admitted
Prices: Normal prices apply for the disabled and helpers
Disabled Toilets: Available
Contact: (01246) 292622 (Bookings are not necessary)

Travelling Supporters' Information:
Routes: The Stadium is located just by the side of the A61 Urstone-Dronfield bypass, just to the north of Dronfield. Take the A61 to Dronfield and exit at the roundabout onto the B6057, heading into Dronfield on Sheffield Road. The entrance to the stadium is clearly visible on the right hand side of the road, just before the junction with Wreakes Lane.

SHEPSHED DYNAMO FC |

Founded: 1994	**Colours:** Black & White striped shirts with Black shorts
Former Names: None	**Telephone Nº:** (01509) 650992
Nickname: 'Dynamo'	**Fax Number:** (01509) 650992
Ground: The Dovecote Stadium, Butthole Lane,	**Ground Capacity:** 2,050
Shepshed LE12 9BN	**Seating Capacity:** 570
Record Attendance: 2,500 (1996/97 season)	**Web Site:** www.shepsheddynamo.co.uk
Pitch Size: 113 × 71 yards	

GENERAL INFORMATION

Car Parking: At the ground
Coach Parking: At the ground
Nearest Railway Station: Loughborough (5½ miles)
Club Shop: At the ground
Opening Times: Matchdays only
Telephone Nº: –

GROUND INFORMATION

Away Supporters' Entrances & Sections:
No usual segregation

ADMISSION INFO (2011/2012 PRICES)

Adult Standing: £7.00
Adult Seating: £7.00
Senior Citizen Standing/Seating: £5.00
Under-16s Standing/Seating: £2.00
Programme Price: £1.50

DISABLED INFORMATION

Wheelchairs: Accommodated
Helpers: Admitted
Prices: Concessionary prices are charged for the disabled and helpers
Disabled Toilets: Available
Contact: (01509) 650992   (Bookings are not necessary)

Travelling Supporters' Information:
Routes: Exit the M1 at Junction 23 and take the A512 towards Ashby. Turn right at the first set of traffic lights and head north into Shepshed along Leicester Road for approximately 1 mile. Turn right into Forest Street at the mini-roundabout by the Texaco petrol station then, after the road bends round left, turn right into Butthole Lane opposite the Black Swan Public House. The ground is immediately on the left.

STAMFORD FC

Founded: 1896
Former Names: None
Nickname: 'The Daniels'
Ground: Kettering Road, Stamford   PE9 2JS
Record Attendance: 4,200 (vs Kettering – 1953)
Pitch Size: 112 × 72 yards

Colours: Red shirts and shorts
Telephone N°: (01780) 763079
Fax Number: (01780) 763079
Ground Capacity: 3,500
Seating Capacity: 250
Web site: www.stamfordafc.net

GENERAL INFORMATION
Car Parking: At the ground
Coach Parking: Outside of the ground
Nearest Railway Station: Stamford (Adjacent)
Club Shop: At the ground
Opening Times: Matchdays only
Telephone N°: –

GROUND INFORMATION
Away Supporters' Entrances & Sections:
No usual segregation

ADMISSION INFO (2011/2012 PRICES)
Adult Standing/Seating: £8.00   (Members £6.00)
Senior Citizen Standing/Seating: £5.00   (Members £4.00)
Under-11s Standing/Seating: Free of charge
Ages 11 to 15 Standing/Seating: £2.00
Programme Price: £1.80

DISABLED INFORMATION
Wheelchairs: 5 spaces in total available in the Main Stand
Helpers: Admitted
Prices: Normal prices apply
Disabled Toilets: None
Contact: (01780) 763079

Travelling Supporters' Information:
Routes: From the North: Exit the A1 onto the slip road with the A43 and turn left at the junction. The ground is situated on the left after about 1 mile; From the South: Leave the A1 at the first roundabout approaching Stamford (2nd exit) and take the B1081 towards Stamford. Continue into the built up area then turn left onto the A43 (Kettering) road and the ground is on the right hand side after 200 yards; From the South: Exit the A1 onto the first slip road for Stamford (B1081) then turn left at the junction towards Stamford. Continue into the built up area then turn left onto the A43 (Kettering) and the ground is on the right hand side after 200 yards.

SUTTON COLDFIELD TOWN FC |

Founded: 1879
Former Names: Sutton Coldfield FC
Nickname: 'The Royals'
Ground: Central Ground, Coles Lane, Sutton Coldfield, B72 1NL
Record Attendance: 2,029 (1980/81 season)
Pitch Size: 109 × 71 yards

Colours: Blue shirts and shorts
Telephone Nº: (0121) 354-2997
Fax Number: (0121) 354-2997
Ground Capacity: 2,500
Seating Capacity: 200
Web Site: www.pitchero.com/clubs/suttoncoldfieldtownfc

GENERAL INFORMATION

Car Parking: At the ground
Coach Parking: At the ground
Nearest Railway Station: Sutton Coldfield (¾ mile)
Club Shop: None
Opening Times: –
Telephone Nº: –

GROUND INFORMATION

Away Supporters' Entrances & Sections:
No usual segregation

ADMISSION INFO (2011/2012 PRICES)

Adult Standing: £7.00
Adult Seating: £7.00
Senior Citizen/Junior Standing: £4.00
Senior Citizen/Junior Seating: £4.00
Programme Price: £1.50

DISABLED INFORMATION

Wheelchairs: Accommodated
Helpers: Admitted
Prices: Normal prices apply for the disabled and helpers
Disabled Toilets: Available
Contact: (0121) 354-2997   (Bookings are necessary)

Travelling Supporters' Information:
Routes: Exit the M42 at Junction 9 and take the A4097 Minworth road. At Minworth roundabout, follow signs for Walmley Village and turn right at the T-junction onto the B4148 Walmley Road. Take the 3rd turning on the left into Wylde Green Road, pass over the canal and the railway bridge then turn right into East View Road which becomes Coles Road as the road bends around. The entrance to the ground is on the right between a gap in the houses.

Evo-Stik League Premier Division 2010/2011 Season	Ashton United	Bradford Park Avenue	Burscough	Buxton	Chasetown	Colwyn Bay	FC Halifax Town	FC United of Manchester	Frickley Athletic	Hucknall Town	Kendal Town	Marine	Matlock Town	Mickleover Sports	Nantwich Town	North Ferriby United	Northwich Victoria	Ossett Town	Retford United	Stocksbridge Park Steels	Whitby Town	Worksop Town
Ashton United	■	1-3	1-0	2-1	2-3	3-0	0-3	1-0	3-6	4-0	1-2	1-0	3-1	2-3	2-4	0-1	2-1	0-1	1-0	3-1	1-3	3-1
Bradford Park Avenue	2-0	■	3-1	4-1	2-1	1-4	1-3	4-1	2-3	6-0	5-2	2-1	3-1	1-0	1-0	1-2	2-2	0-1	2-0	3-0	1-1	4-0
Burscough	4-1	2-3	■	1-2	0-3	0-0	0-2	0-2	3-0	3-0	2-4	1-2	0-3	3-2	3-1	2-2	0-0	0-1	0-1	0-2	1-0	3-1
Buxton	1-1	1-1	1-0	■	2-0	0-0	2-1	2-2	7-1	4-0	3-0	2-1	1-3	1-2	2-1	0-0	2-2	2-0	7-0	0-0	2-0	0-1
Chasetown	2-1	5-0	5-0	0-1	■	2-2	2-1	2-0	2-0	1-0	0-1	0-1	2-1	2-3	2-2	2-2	1-0	1-0	6-0	0-2	1-1	2-6
Colwyn Bay	0-3	2-2	2-1	2-1	1-0	■	2-1	3-1	4-0	2-0	2-1	0-3	0-1	1-1	2-0	0-2	0-6	3-1	1-0	3-4	2-0	2-1
FC Halifax Town	1-0	1-0	3-2	2-1	3-2	1-1	■	4-1	3-1	4-0	3-0	1-0	2-2	1-1	3-1	0-2	1-1	8-1	3-0	5-1	5-1	0-0
FC United of Manchester	2-1	2-0	3-1	1-2	4-2	0-1	0-1	■	4-1	4-1	1-2	2-1	1-5	0-0	1-0	2-0	1-0	4-1	5-1	1-4	4-0	2-1
Frickley Athletic	0-0	2-2	0-1	2-2	2-1	0-1	0-0	0-0	■	1-0	0-2	2-3	0-1	1-0	3-0	0-1	2-1	0-1	1-2	1-1	0-0	1-0
Hucknall Town	0-0	2-2	2-2	0-1	2-2	0-1	1-2	1-2	2-0	■	4-3	0-3	2-2	1-0	3-1	3-2	0-2	3-3	5-3	2-2	1-2	1-2
Kendal Town	1-0	4-1	1-2	1-1	4-0	1-4	2-4	3-2	1-0	0-0	■	2-1	1-0	1-2	2-1	2-5	1-1	5-4	4-1	2-3	2-1	2-1
Marine	4-0	1-0	2-2	1-2	2-0	1-3	0-6	0-2	1-1	1-1	2-0	■	2-4	1-2	4-3	2-3	3-1	4-3	2-0	5-4	1-3	2-4
Matlock Town	1-1	0-1	2-1	1-3	3-4	3-0	1-2	1-2	1-0	1-2	3-1	0-1	■	1-2	4-2	2-1	1-1	2-0	4-2	1-0	2-2	1-0
Mickleover Sports	0-1	1-3	2-1	2-4	1-3	4-0	2-3	2-0	3-0	1-1	1-3	0-0	1-0	■	6-6	3-4	2-3	2-4	4-1	2-0	2-4	0-1
Nantwich Town	0-2	0-1	3-2	1-1	0-4	2-1	0-6	1-4	4-3	1-2	5-3	1-1	2-3	0-0	■	2-1	2-1	2-1	1-0	4-2	3-1	1-2
North Ferriby United	3-2	1-2	2-1	2-0	0-1	1-3	0-3	1-1	4-0	3-0	4-1	0-1	3-1	4-2	1-2	■	1-2	4-0	0-1	2-1	6-0	3-0
Northwich Victoria	1-0	2-1	3-0	4-2	1-1	0-1	0-3	1-0	0-1	4-0	1-6	4-3	2-3	1-0	1-1	1-1	■	0-1	4-1	0-1	2-0	3-1
Ossett Town	0-5	0-6	1-2	0-1	2-4	2-3	0-0	0-3	1-2	1-6	0-0	0-2	0-0	1-2	0-5	0-0	0-2	■	2-1	3-5	0-4	2-3
Retford United	1-2	0-0	0-2	1-3	0-4	3-5	0-2	0-4	1-3	2-5	2-1	0-3	0-4	0-2	3-2	1-2	0-1	0-2	■	0-0	0-3	0-3
Stocksbridge Park Steels	0-0	0-1	2-4	1-4	2-0	0-1	3-5	1-2	1-1	1-0	2-1	1-3	3-1	7-3	3-1	0-1	3-0	3-0	3-2	■	2-1	2-3
Whitby Town	2-1	1-2	2-2	1-0	0-1	2-2	1-5	0-1	2-2	1-0	2-2	1-1	1-2	3-2	3-1	0-1	2-4	3-1	2-1	2-0	■	0-3
Worksop Town	3-0	3-3	1-1	3-0	2-0	0-1	1-1	1-2	1-1	2-0	1-2	1-2	2-1	2-0	0-0	4-1	2-0	1-4	1-0	2-1	5-0	■

Evo-Stik League Division One North 2010/2011 Season	AFC Fylde	Bamber Bridge	Cammell Laird	Chester	Chorley	Clitheroe	Curzon Ashton	Durham City	Garforth Town	Harrogate Railway Athletic	Lancaster City	Leigh Genesis	Mossley	Ossett Albion	Prescot Cables	Radcliffe Borough	Salford City	Skelmersdale United	Trafford	Wakefield	Warrington Town	Witton Albion	Woodley Sports
AFC Fylde	■	0-2	1-1	1-3	3-0	0-1	3-1	4-2	1-0	5-2	4-1	4-0	0-2	2-0	2-1	5-2	3-1	2-3	3-2	4-0	3-0	1-1	3-2
Bamber Bridge	3-2	■	1-0	0-5	1-1	1-2	2-0	1-0	1-1	2-3	2-1	3-0	2-2	5-0	0-1	2-1	2-2	0-0	1-2	4-1	1-1	3-3	2-1
Cammell Laird	0-3	2-4	■	1-2	1-1	3-0	2-5	4-2	3-2	4-8	2-1	0-0	1-2	5-1	2-2	4-0	3-3	0-2	1-0	3-2	2-3	0-1	1-2
Chester	2-2	2-0	2-0	■	1-2	5-0	2-2	3-1	2-0	3-2	3-0	1-1	3-0	6-0	1-1	2-3	3-1	4-0	6-0	3-1	2-2	0-0	3-0
Chorley	0-0	2-0	3-0	0-1	■	1-1	1-0	5-0	1-2	1-2	2-1	3-1	2-1	2-1	5-2	4-1	1-0	2-0	0-1	2-1	0-3	2-2	6-0
Clitheroe	2-2	1-1	3-3	0-5	0-2	■	0-3	4-1	3-3	3-3	2-0	6-0	5-0	2-2	2-0	2-0	4-5	2-2	2-3	2-3	2-2	3-1	0-1
Curzon Ashton	1-1	2-2	3-0	3-1	2-6	0-0	■	4-1	4-1	5-2	0-1	2-0	1-0	7-0	1-1	3-0	1-0	2-3	3-2	3-2	0-2	2-0	3-1
Durham City	1-3	2-1	3-3	0-3	0-3	1-1	1-1	■	0-0	1-1	5-0	3-1	3-2	4-2	1-1	0-2	6-2	3-3	0-2	3-1	1-3	1-1	6-2
Garforth Town	1-1	0-1	0-1	2-1	1-1	0-1	2-0	1-1	■	2-6	2-4	3-1	2-1	4-0	0-0	2-2	2-1	0-3	2-1	4-0	3-0	0-0	4-3
Harrogate Railway Ath.	2-3	0-1	5-1	1-4	3-2	1-4	1-2	4-1	1-4	■	2-3	0-1	4-3	2-3	0-0	2-1	0-1	2-4	3-2	0-1	1-3	1-1	0-2
Lancaster City	2-0	3-1	1-0	2-1	0-2	1-2	0-2	4-0	5-2	4-1	■	6-0	2-0	4-1	1-2	0-1	0-0	1-0	2-2	2-1	0-4	2-0	2-0
Leigh Genesis	0-1	1-3	1-3	1-1	1-2	1-2	1-2	0-4	1-0	1-2	0-0	■	1-3	3-3	1-1	2-1	0-3	2-3	3-2	0-1	3-3	0-8	2-3
Mossley	2-0	0-1	1-2	0-1	1-3	3-2	1-1	0-2	2-1	3-0	2-4	0-2	■	4-0	1-2	1-1	1-3	1-4	6-0	3-0	1-1	3-3	0-0
Ossett Albion	2-5	2-6	3-2	0-3	2-2	1-1	2-3	2-1	1-1	2-2	0-4	2-1	1-1	■	1-3	3-3	6-2	2-5	2-0	1-1	1-3	1-3	2-5
Prescot Cables	0-1	0-2	1-1	0-1	0-2	1-2	2-1	3-4	1-1	1-2	0-4	4-0	1-5	2-2	■	2-0	1-2	1-4	2-2	0-1	3-1	1-2	2-2
Radcliffe Borough	1-1	1-0	0-2	2-2	1-2	2-3	0-0	0-3	2-5	1-0	2-2	3-2	0-4	4-1	1-1	■	1-1	1-4	5-3	0-0	1-0	1-2	2-3
Salford City	3-1	1-2	1-0	0-4	0-2	2-3	0-1	4-0	1-2	1-1	2-2	2-0	2-2	1-0	0-0	1-2	■	0-5	2-2	2-1	1-2	1-0	1-1
Skelmersdale United	1-3	6-0	8-0	0-1	1-1	1-2	1-1	2-0	1-0	1-0	2-1	4-0	4-0	7-2	3-0	2-2	2-2	■	5-2	2-1	1-2	6-1	1-0
Trafford	1-4	0-2	4-1	0-2	0-4	1-1	0-2	3-1	2-2	5-2	1-0	4-1	1-4	3-1	1-2	2-0	2-1	0-3	■	2-0	1-2	1-1	0-1
Wakefield	0-1	1-0	2-1	1-2	2-2	1-0	0-1	1-4	3-2	3-2	2-0	3-0	3-2	1-1	6-0	1-2	1-2	0-2	3-0	■	1-1	1-1	1-0
Warrington Town	1-1	1-1	0-1	1-1	1-0	0-2	0-1	3-1	2-2	4-0	2-1	2-1	1-1	2-0	2-2	1-2	1-2	0-1	3-1	1-1	■	2-0	1-1
Witton Albion	3-4	2-0	3-0	2-3	0-0	2-0	1-1	1-1	1-0	2-2	0-5	5-1	2-0	5-0	3-1	3-3	0-1	0-1	2-5	3-1	1-1	■	2-2
Woodley Sports	2-0	2-1	2-0	1-1	2-2	0-2	3-1	1-0	2-1	2-4	2-1	1-1	3-4	2-1	3-1	4-0	2-3	2-4	2-2	1-1	0-0	0-1	■

Evo-Stik League Division One South 2010/2011 Season	Barwell	Belper Town	Brigg Town	Carlton Town	Glapwell	Goole	Grantham Town	Kidsgrove Athletic	Leek Town	Lincoln United	Loughborough Dynamo	Market Drayton Town	Newcastle Town	Quorn	Rainworth Miners Welfare	Romulus	Rushall Olympic	Sheffield	Shepshed Dynamo	Spalding United	Stamford	Sutton Coldfield Town
Barwell	■	1-0	3-2	1-2	1-0	4-1	2-1	2-1	2-0	0-4	4-0	4-0	1-1	3-2	3-0	3-1	2-0	3-0	3-3	1-0	2-1	1-0
Belper Town	0-1	■	0-1	0-0	2-1	0-1	0-2	0-1	3-5	1-1	1-0	5-1	0-5	1-5	2-2	4-1	1-2	2-3	2-1	5-0	4-5	1-4
Brigg Town	0-2	1-2	■	1-0	2-1	3-0	1-1	2-0	1-1	0-2	1-7	4-3	0-2	4-0	1-1	2-1	4-3	0-0	2-1	2-1	3-2	1-0
Carlton Town	4-2	0-3	1-2	■	0-0	4-5	2-2	3-3	1-0	3-0	4-0	5-2	0-0	0-0	2-1	0-1	0-0	2-0	7-2	4-0	3-1	2-0
Glapwell	0-1	0-3	0-4	1-0	■	3-0	7-1	3-0	2-1	4-1	1-2	3-1	1-3	3-0	2-0	5-0	3-5	4-2	1-2	2-1	1-0	0-2
Goole	1-4	0-1	1-3	3-6	1-0	■	2-1	1-1	4-2	5-1	0-1	1-3	4-4	2-1	5-1	1-2	1-0	2-5	4-1	4-1	1-0	1-2
Grantham Town	5-2	2-1	2-0	1-0	0-0	1-2	■	2-1	2-0	1-1	2-1	1-2	3-0	1-1	1-3	1-0	1-0	3-1	2-2	0-0	4-1	0-3
Kidsgrove Athletic	0-2	4-2	1-2	2-5	4-0	5-3	1-2	■	3-2	1-0	2-0	3-1	1-2	2-1	4-0	5-1	2-0	2-2	0-0	3-1	4-3	1-2
Leek Town	2-3	0-2	0-1	2-1	0-2	4-1	2-1	0-1	■	4-3	3-3	4-0	0-1	1-0	2-3	0-2	1-2	0-2	2-0	2-2	1-0	1-2
Lincoln United	3-2	1-2	2-3	0-2	3-2	0-0	2-5	2-2	1-1	■	6-1	1-1	1-1	0-0	3-0	2-0	0-1	4-2	1-1	6-1	2-0	1-3
Loughborough Dyn.	0-3	5-4	2-2	1-4	1-4	4-1	1-1	0-3	2-3	6-0	■	0-1	3-1	2-1	1-2	1-1	2-5	1-3	5-1	5-0	2-2	1-2
Market Drayton Town	2-2	2-4	2-2	0-2	0-1	2-1	0-3	0-1	2-1	2-2	4-0	■	1-8	0-2	1-2	2-4	0-2	3-1	6-0	3-0	0-3	3-4
Newcastle Town	4-1	2-3	1-2	2-1	3-0	3-1	1-1	3-0	1-2	3-0	3-1	2-1	■	1-1	4-1	3-1	5-2	1-1	5-2	3-1	4-0	1-2
Quorn	1-2	2-0	0-3	2-1	2-3	3-3	1-2	3-3	0-1	1-2	4-1	1-1	0-0	■	3-1	2-3	1-0	1-3	0-0	3-0	0-1	2-1
Rainworth Miners W.	0-2	0-2	3-2	2-2	1-1	0-1	1-2	0-1	2-1	2-3	1-2	0-2	0-2	1-2	■	3-5	3-1	0-0	3-2	2-0	2-2	1-2
Romulus	2-1	2-0	0-1	0-1	2-2	0-5	0-1	1-0	2-2	5-1	2-0	2-0	0-2	3-3	3-0	■	0-0	0-2	4-2	3-2	0-1	2-1
Rushall Olympic	0-1	3-2	2-0	2-1	2-2	3-1	1-0	2-0	2-0	2-1	0-2	2-1	2-3	0-1	2-0	0-1	■	5-0	2-0	6-0	1-0	3-0
Sheffield	0-3	1-1	5-0	1-1	1-3	2-1	1-2	2-4	4-3	1-1	1-1	1-1	1-4	2-2	1-4	1-3	2-3	■	3-2	2-1	3-2	2-1
Shepshed Dynamo	1-1	1-0	0-2	1-3	0-5	3-3	0-1	1-4	0-2	0-2	0-1	0-2	0-2	1-1	3-1	1-2	0-2	1-2	■	5-1	1-4	0-4
Spalding United	1-2	0-1	0-4	0-4	0-2	1-2	0-2	1-6	0-4	2-1	2-2	2-4	3-3	1-1	0-3	0-7	0-3	3-2	2-1	■	0-4	1-1
Stamford	0-1	2-2	2-3	2-2	2-1	1-1	1-1	0-4	2-1	1-2	1-0	1-3	2-3	0-0	1-1	0-3	2-2	1-1	6-1	■		1-1
Sutton Coldfield Tn.	1-0	3-1	1-1	2-3	2-5	7-2	1-2	0-2	6-1	4-1	3-2	3-2	1-2	1-1	5-1	1-1	1-2	4-2	3-1	1-1	2-1	■

The Evo-Stik League
Premier Division
Season 2010/2011

FC Halifax Town	42	30	8	4	108	36	98
Colwyn Bay	42	24	7	11	67	56	79
Bradford Park Avenue	42	23	8	11	84	55	77
FC United of Manchester	42	24	4	14	76	53	76
North Ferriby United	42	22	7	13	78	51	73
Buxton	42	20	10	12	71	52	70
Kendal Town	42	21	5	16	80	77	68
Marine	42	20	7	15	74	64	67
Worksop Town	42	21	6	15	72	54	66
Chasetown	42	20	6	16	76	59	66
Matlock Town	42	20	6	16	74	59	66
Northwich Victoria	42	18	9	15	66	55	63
Stocksbridge Park Steels	42	17	6	19	75	75	57
Ashton United	42	16	5	21	57	62	53
Mickleover Sports	42	15	7	20	70	76	52
Whitby Town	42	14	9	19	58	77	51
Nantwich Town	42	13	7	22	68	90	46
Frickley Athletic	42	11	11	20	43	68	44
Burscough	42	12	7	23	56	73	43
Hucknall Town	42	11	10	21	57	80	43
Ossett Town	42	9	5	28	45	103	32
Retford United	42	5	2	35	31	111	17

Worksop Town had 3 points deducted.
Burscough were reprieved from relegation due to Ilkeston Town folding in the Conference North earlier in the season.

Promotion Play-offs

Bradford Park Avenue 0	FC United of Manchester 2
Colwyn Bay 2	North Ferriby United 0

Colwyn Bay 1	FC United of Manchester 0

Promoted: FC Halifax Town and Colwyn Bay

Relegated: Hucknall Town, Ossett Town and Retford United

The Evo-Stik League Division One North

Season 2010/2011

Chester	44	29	10	5	107	36	97
Skelmersdale United	44	30	7	7	117	48	97
Chorley	44	25	11	8	87	43	86
Curzon Ashton	44	25	10	9	85	49	85
AFC Fylde	44	24	9	11	91	59	81
Clitheroe	44	19	13	12	82	70	70
Bamber Bridge	44	20	10	14	70	60	70
Lancaster City	44	21	5	18	80	61	68
Warrington Town	44	18	16	10	70	50	67
Witton Albion	44	15	17	12	75	63	62
Woodley Sports	44	17	11	16	71	75	62
Salford City	44	17	11	16	68	73	62
Garforth Town	44	13	13	18	67	71	52
Trafford	44	15	7	22	73	92	52
Mossley	44	14	9	21	75	77	51
Wakefield	44	14	8	22	55	74	50
Durham City	44	13	10	21	75	92	48
Radcliffe Borough	44	12	12	20	60	89	48
Cammell Laird	44	13	8	23	66	94	47
Harrogate Railway Athletic	44	13	7	24	82	103	46
Prescot Cables	44	9	15	20	52	79	42
Ossett Albion	44	6	11	27	60	134	26
Leigh Genesis	44	5	8	31	39	112	23

Warrington Town and Ossett Albion both had 3 points deducted.
Durham City had 1 point deducted.
Leigh Genesis folded at the end of the season.

Promotion Play-offs

Skelmersdale United 0	AFC Fylde		1
Chorley 2	Curzon Ashton		1
Chorley 2	AFC Fylde		0

Promoted: Chester and Chorley

The Evo-Stik League Division One South

Season 2010/2011

Barwell	42	30	4	8	84	46	94
Newcastle Town	42	27	9	6	104	48	90
Rushall Olympic	42	26	3	13	78	45	81
Brigg Town	42	24	8	10	74	58	80
Grantham Town	42	23	10	9	69	48	79
Sutton Coldfield Town	42	23	6	13	89	60	75
Kidsgrove Athletic	42	23	6	13	88	59	75
Carlton Town	42	21	10	11	88	50	73
Glapwell	42	21	6	15	82	58	69
Romulus	42	20	7	15	71	65	67
Sheffield	42	15	10	17	73	86	55
Lincoln United	42	14	12	16	70	77	54
Goole	42	16	6	20	79	93	54
Belper Town	42	16	5	21	70	74	53
Quorn	42	11	14	17	57	61	47
Leek Town	42	14	5	23	64	74	47
Loughborough Dynamo	42	13	7	22	72	89	46
Market Drayton Town	42	13	5	24	67	91	44
Stamford	42	10	12	20	62	74	42
Rainworth Miners Welfare	42	11	7	24	53	85	40
Shepshed Dynamo	42	4	9	29	44	103	21
Spalding United	42	3	7	32	33	127	16

Glapwell resigned from the League at the end of the season.

Promotion Play-offs

Newcastle Town 0	Grantham Town 3
Rushall Olympic 3	Brigg Town 0
Rushall Olympic 2	Grantham Town 0

Promoted: Barwell and Rushall Olympic
Relegated: Spalding United

F.A. Trophy 2010/2011

Qualifying 1	AFC Hornchurch	2	Brentwood Town	1
Qualifying 1	AFC Totton	5	AFC Hayes	0
Qualifying 1	Almondsbury Town	1	Didcot Town	0
Qualifying 1	Arlesey Town	0	Ramsgate	0
Qualifying 1	Ashford Town (Middlesex)	6	North Greenford United	2
Qualifying 1	Banbury United	1	Wimborne Town	1
Qualifying 1	Bideford	4	Tiverton Town	2
Qualifying 1	Biggleswade Town	0	Billericay Town	1
Qualifying 1	Bognor Regis Town	1	Croydon Athletic	0
Qualifying 1	Bridgwater Town	1	Stourbridge	3
Qualifying 1	Burnham	0	Brackley Town	0
Qualifying 1	Burscough	0	Clitheroe	2
Qualifying 1	Bury Town	2	Barton Rovers	0
Qualifying 1	Buxton	1	Stocksbridge Park Steels	2
Qualifying 1	Cambridge City	1	Aveley	0
Qualifying 1	Cammell Laird	1	Witton Albion	2
Qualifying 1	Canvey Island	1	AFC Sudbury	2
Qualifying 1	Carlton Town	1	Rushall Olympic	1
Qualifying 1	Carshalton Athletic	2	Ilford	0
Qualifying 1	Chesham United	1	Salisbury City	1
Qualifying 1	Chorley	1	Quorn	0
Qualifying 1	Cinderford Town	2	Hungerford Town	2
Qualifying 1	Cirencester Town	3	Halesowen Town	0
Qualifying 1	Colwyn Bay	2	Bradford Park Avenue	0
Qualifying 1	Cray Wanderers	2	Wingate & Finchley	1
Qualifying 1	Curzon Ashton	3	Skelmersdale United	1
Qualifying 1	Dulwich Hamlet	2	Hastings United	2
Qualifying 1	Durham City	0	FC Halifax Town	2
Qualifying 1	Enfield Town	2	Walton Casuals	1
Qualifying 1	Evesham United	1	Frome Town	0
Qualifying 1	FC United of Manchester	5	Newcastle Town	0
Qualifying 1	Faversham Town	1	Kingstonian	2
Qualifying 1	Fleet Town	0	Godalming Town	2
Qualifying 1	Folkestone Invicta	4	Worthing	2
Qualifying 1	Glapwell	2	Stamford	0
Qualifying 1	Great Wakering Rovers	1	Thamesmead Town	2
Qualifying 1	Harlow Town	3	Bedford Town	2
Qualifying 1	Harrogate Railway Athletic	2	Ossett Albion	1
Qualifying 1	Harrow Borough	0	Hendon	1
Qualifying 1	Hednesford Town	1	Whitby Town	2
Qualifying 1	Hemel Hempstead Town	2	Rugby Town	3
Qualifying 1	Horsham	3	Redbridge	0
Qualifying 1	Kendal Town	3	Frickley Athletic	0
Qualifying 1	Lancaster City	4	Ossett Town	2
Qualifying 1	Maidstone United	2	Burgess Hill Town	0
Qualifying 1	Margate	5	Whitehawk	1
Qualifying 1	Marine	2	Ashton United	2
Qualifying 1	Matlock Town	10	Bedworth United	0
Qualifying 1	Mickleover Sports	2	Hucknall Town	1

Round	Home	Score	Away	Score	
Qualifying 1	Market Drayton Town	1	Worksop Town	1	
Qualifying 1	North Ferriby United	0	Bamber Bridge	2	
Qualifying 1	Nantwich Town	6	Prescot Cables	2	
Qualifying 1	Needham Market	2	Lowestoft Town	2	
Qualifying 1	Northwich Victoria	0	Lincoln United	0	
Qualifying 1	Oxford City	1	Daventry Town	4	
Qualifying 1	Paulton Rovers	3	North Leigh	3	
Qualifying 1	Radcliffe Borough	1	Garforth Town	1	
Qualifying 1	Retford United	2	Romulus	2	
Qualifying 1	Sheffield	1	Chasetown	1	
Qualifying 1	Shepshed Dynamo	1	Mossley	4	
Qualifying 1	Slough Town	1	Chippenham Town	1	
Qualifying 1	Soham Town Rangers	1	Grays Athletic	2	
Qualifying 1	Sutton United	3	Tooting & Mitcham United	1	
Qualifying 1	Swindon Supermarine	4	Beaconsfield SYCOB	2	
Qualifying 1	Tonbridge Angels	3	Concord Rangers	2	
Qualifying 1	Truro City	1	Bishop's Cleeve	0	
Qualifying 1	Uxbridge	4	Abingdon United	1	
Qualifying 1	Waltham Forest	0	Romford	2	
Qualifying 1	Wealdstone	2	Potters Bar Town	2	
Qualifying 1	Weymouth	2	Bashley	1	
Qualifying 1	Windsor & Eton	1	Aylesbury	1	
Qualifying 1	Woodford United	1	Leamington	3	
Replay	Ashton United	1	Marine	3	
Replay	Aylesbury	1	Windsor & Eton	2	
Replay	Brackley Town	4	Burnham	0	
Replay	Chasetown	3	Sheffield	1	
Replay	Chippenham Town	4	Slough Town	1	
Replay	Garforth Town	1	Radcliffe Borough	2	
Replay	Hastings United	1	Dulwich Hamlet	2	
Replay	Hungerford Town	1	Cinderford Town	2	(aet)
Replay	Lincoln United	2	Northwich Victoria	3	
Replay	Lowestoft Town	6	Needham Market	2	
Replay	North Leigh	1	Paulton Rovers	2	
Replay	Potters Bar Town	1	Wealdstone	3	
Replay	Ramsgate	2	Arlesey Town	3	(aet)
Replay	Romulus	2	Retford United	1	
Replay	Rushall Olympic	4	Carlton Town	1	
Replay	Salisbury City	2	Chesham United	1	
Replay	Wimborne Town	1	Banbury United	3	(aet)
Replay	Worksop Town	1	Market Drayton Town	0	
Qualifying 2	AFC Sudbury	5	Hendon	1	
Qualifying 2	AFC Totton	1	Romford	3	
Qualifying 2	Arlesey Town	2	Uxbridge	2	
Qualifying 2	Ashford Town (Middlesex)	2	Bury Town	1	
Qualifying 2	Bideford	1	Dulwich Hamlet	0	
Qualifying 2	Billericay Town	2	Banbury United	1	
Qualifying 2	Bognor Regis Town	1	Godalming Town	1	
Qualifying 2	Brackley Town	4	Windsor & Eton	0	
Qualifying 2	Chippenham Town	1	Lowestoft Town	1	
Qualifying 2	Chorley	3	Marine	1	

Qualifying 2	Cirencester Town	2	Weymouth	1	
Qualifying 2	Cray Wanderers	1	Maidstone United	2	
Qualifying 2	Curzon Ashton	2	FC Halifax Town	1	
Qualifying 2	Daventry Town	1	Cambridge City	2	
Qualifying 2	Evesham United	0	Sutton United	1	
Qualifying 2	FC United of Manchester	2	Colwyn Bay	1	
Qualifying 2	Folkestone Invicta	0	Thamesmead Town	0	
Qualifying 2	Grays Athletic	2	Cinderford Town	1	
Qualifying 2	Harlow Town	2	Carshalton Athletic	0	
Qualifying 2	Kendal Town	1	Matlock Town	1	
Qualifying 2	Kingstonian	3	Wealdstone	5	
Qualifying 2	Leamington	3	Bamber Bridge	0	
Qualifying 2	Lowestoft Town	3	Chippenham Town	1	(aet)
Qualifying 2	Margate	1	AFC Hornchurch	2	
Qualifying 2	Mickleover Sports	2	Chasetown	5	
Qualifying 2	Mossley	2	Nantwich Town	3	
Qualifying 2	Northwich Victoria	4	Glapwell	0	
Qualifying 2	Paulton Rovers	4	Swindon Supermarine	5	
Qualifying 2	Radcliffe Borough	1	Witton Albion	1	
Qualifying 2	Romulus	1	Harrogate Railway Athletic	2	
Qualifying 2	Rushall Olympic	0	Stourbridge	1	
Qualifying 2	Salisbury City	2	Almondsbury Town	1	
Qualifying 2	Stocksbridge Park Steels	3	Rugby Town	2	
Qualifying 2	Tonbridge Angels	2	Enfield Town	0	
Qualifying 2	Truro City	2	Horsham	0	
Qualifying 2	Whitby Town	3	Clitheroe	1	
Qualifying 2	Worksop Town	2	Lancaster City	1	
Replay	Godalming Town	2	Bognor Regis Town	5	
Replay	Matlock Town	1	Kendal Town	2	
Replay	Thamesmead Town	1	Folkestone Invicta	3	
Replay	Uxbridge	4	Arlesey Town	2	
Replay	Witton Albion	3	Radcliffe Borough	1	
Qualifying 3	AFC Telford United	2	Corby Town	1	
Qualifying 3	Alfreton Town	4	Kendal Town	0	
Qualifying 3	Basingstoke Town	2	Havant & Waterlooville	2	
Qualifying 3	Bideford	0	AFC Hornchurch	3	
Qualifying 3	Blyth Spartans	1	Stafford Rangers	0	
Qualifying 3	Bognor Regis Town	2	Hampton & Richmond Borough	2	
Qualifying 3	Boreham Wood	3	Romford	0	
Qualifying 3	Boston United	2	Gainsborough Trinity	1	
Qualifying 3	Brackley Town	0	Wealdstone	1	
Qualifying 3	Braintree Town	2	Farnborough	0	
Qualifying 3	Bishop's Stortford	1	Ashford Town (Middlesex)	2	
Qualifying 3	Chorley	0	Guiseley	1	
Qualifying 3	Cirencester Town	2	Grays Athletic	2	
Qualifying 3	Curzon Ashton	2	Solihull Moors	1	
Qualifying 3	Dover Athletic	1	Woking	2	
Qualifying 3	Droylsden	3	Stourbridge	2	
Qualifying 3	Eastleigh	2	Folkestone Invicta	1	
Qualifying 3	Eastwood Town	2	Cambridge City	0	
Qualifying 3	Ebbsfleet United	4	Bromley	0	

Qualifying 3	FC United of Manchester	1	Hinckley United	2
Qualifying 3	Harlow Town	3	Maidstone United	0
Qualifying 3	Harrogate Railway Athletic	3	Nantwich Town	4
Qualifying 3	Harrogate Town	1	Witton Albion	1
Qualifying 3	Leamington	1	Hyde	2
Qualifying 3	Lewes	1	Salisbury City	3
Qualifying 3	Lowestoft Town	2	Swindon Supermarine	1
Qualifying 3	Maidenhead United	2	Uxbridge	4
Qualifying 3	Nuneaton Town	1	Worcester City	2
Qualifying 3	Redditch United	80	Bye	0
Qualifying 3	St. Albans City	3	Staines Town	1
Qualifying 3	Sutton United	4	Billericay Town	2
Qualifying 3	Thurrock	0	Dartford	2
Qualifying 3	Truro City	1	AFC Sudbury	2
Qualifying 3	Vauxhall Motors (Cheshire)	1	Stalybridge Celtic	3
Qualifying 3	Welling United	1	Tonbridge Angels	0
Qualifying 3	Weston-Super-Mare	1	Dorchester Town	3
Qualifying 3	Whitby Town	2	Northwich Victoria	2
Qualifying 3	Workington	0	Chasetown	0
Qualifying 3	Worksop Town	1	Chelmsford City	0
Qualifying 3	Worksop Town	4	Stocksbridge Park Steels	1
Replay	Chasetown	4	Workington	0
Replay	Grays Athletic	0	Cirencester Town	1
Replay	Hampton & Richmond Borough	2	Bognor Regis Town	0
Replay	Havant & Waterlooville	1	Basingstoke Town	2
Replay	Northwich Victoria	1	Whitby Town	0
Replay	Witton Albion	1	Harrogate Town	2
Round 1	AFC Sudbury	1	Hampton & Richmond Borough	4
Round 1	AFC Wimbledon	3	Braintree Town	0
Round 1	Alfreton Town	3	Hyde	0
Round 1	Ashford Town (Middlesex)	1	AFC Hornchurch	0
Round 1	Barrow	2	Guiseley	3
Round 1	Basingstoke Town	0	Salisbury City	2
Round 1	Blyth Spartans	2	Fleetwood Town	0
Round 1	Cambridge United	2	Forest Green Rovers	1
Round 1	Chasetown	3	Kettering Town	3
Round 1	Cirencester Town	1	Gloucester City	1
Round 1	Crawley Town	3	Dartford	3
Round 1	Curzon Ashton	2	Altrincham	1
	The match was abandoned at half-time due to power failure and a replay was ordered.			
Round 1	Darlington	3	Tamworth	2
Round 1	Dorchester Town	3	St. Albans City	0
Round 1	Droylsden	4	Hinckley United	3
Round 1	Eastbourne Borough	3	Boreham Wood	1
Round 1	Eastleigh	1	Sutton United	0
Round 1	Ebbsfleet United	3	Hayes & Yeading United	1
Round 1	Gateshead	2	Southport	2
Round 1	Grimsby Town	3	Redditch United	0
Round 1	Harlow Town	0	Woking	2
Round 1	Harrogate Town	0	AFC Telford United	3
Round 1	Histon	2	Bath City	3

Round 1	Lowestoft Town	2	Uxbridge	3	
Round 1	Luton Town	0	Welling United	0	
Round 1	Newport County	0	Wealdstone	0	
Round 1	Rushden & Diamonds	1	Eastwood Town	1	
Round 1	Stalybridge Celtic	2	Nantwich Town	1	
Round 1	Worcester City	1	Northwich Victoria	0	
Round 1	Worksop Town	0	Mansfield Town	5	
	Match played at Retford				
Round 1	Wrexham	2	Kidderminster Harriers	0	
Round 1	York City	0	Boston United	1	
Replay	Curzon Ashton	0	Altrincham	2	
Replay	Dartford	1	Crawley Town	0	
Replay	Eastwood Town	4	Rushden & Diamonds	3	(aet)
Replay	Gloucester City	3	Cirencester Town	0	
Replay	Kettering Town	1	Chasetown	2	(aet)
Replay	Southport	0	Gateshead	1	
Replay	Sutton United	0	Eastleigh	4	
Replay	Wealdstone	0	Newport County	1	(aet)
Replay	Welling United	1	Luton Town	2	
Round 2	AFC Telford United	1	Eastwood Town	0	
Round 2	AFC Wimbledon	2	Woking	3	
Round 2	Alfreton Town	3	Cambridge United	3	
Round 2	Ashford Town (Middlesex)	0	Dartford	1	
Round 2	Blyth Spartans	2	Altrincham	1	
Round 2	Boston United	0	Gloucester City	1	
Round 2	Chasetown	2	Grimsby Town	1	
Round 2	Darlington	4	Bath City	1	
Round 2	Dorchester Town	3	Eastbourne Borough	3	
Round 2	Droylsden	1	Ebbsfleet United	0	
Round 2	Eastleigh	3	Worcester City	3	
Round 2	Gateshead	6	Hampton & Richmond Borough	0	
Round 2	Guiseley	2	Stalybridge Celtic	1	
Round 2	Luton Town	4	Uxbridge	0	
Round 2	Mansfield Town	4	Newport County	2	
Round 2	Salisbury City	1	Wrexham	0	
Replay	Cambridge United	3	Alfreton Town	6	(aet)
Replay	Eastbourne Borough	1	Dorchester Town	0	
Replay	Worcester City	1	Eastleigh	4	
Round 3	AFC Telford United	0	Darlington	3	
Round 3	Blyth Spartans	2	Droylsden	2	
Round 3	Eastbourne Borough	1	Guiseley	1	
Round 3	Eastleigh	1	Chasetown	3	
Round 3	Gateshead	3	Dartford	0	
Round 3	Luton Town	1	Gloucester City	0	
Round 3	Mansfield Town	1	Alfreton Town	1	
Round 3	Woking	0	Salisbury City	2	
Replay	Alfreton Town	1	Mansfield Town	2	
Replay	Droylsden	0	Blyth Spartans	4	
Replay	Guiseley	2	Eastbourne Borough	1	

Round 4	Blyth Spartans	0	Gateshead	2	
Round 4	Chasetown	2	Mansfield Town	2	
Round 4	Darlington	2	Salisbury City	1	
Round 4	Guiseley	0	Luton Town	1	
Replay	Mansfield Town	3	Chasetown	1	
Semi-finals					
1st leg	Darlington	3	Gateshead	2	
2nd leg	Gateshead	0	Darlington	0	
	Darlington won 3-2 on aggregate.				
1st leg	Mansfield Town	1	Luton Town	0	
2nd leg	Luton Town	1	Mansfield Town	1	(aet)
	Mansfield Town won 2-1 on aggregate				
FINAL	Darlington	1	Mansfield Town	0	

Cup Statistics provided by:

www.soccerdata.com

85

F.A. Vase 2010/2011

Round	Home	Score	Away	Score	Note
Round 1	AFC Dunstable	3	Colney Heath	1	
Round 1	AFC Emley	3	Runcorn Linnets	1	
Round 1	AFC Liverpool	3	Hallam	0	
Round 1	Atherton Laburnum Rovers	2	Runcorn Town	3	
Round 1	Aylesbury United	4	Hertford Town	3	(aet)
Round 1	Baldock Town Letchworth	0	Holyport	1	
Round 1	Barking	1	Flackwell Heath	2	
Round 1	Bedlington Terriers	0	Spennymoor Town	1	
Round 1	Bemerton Heath Harlequins	5	Lydney Town	2	(aet)
Round 1	Billingham Town	3	Ashington	4	(aet)
Round 1	Binfield	3	Hillingdon Borough	2	
Round 1	Bishop Auckland	3	Billingham Synthonia	4	(aet)
Round 1	Bishop Sutton	2	Keynsham Town	2	(aet)
Round 1	Blaby & Whetstone Athletic	2	Westfields	5	
Round 1	Bloxwich United	5	Pilkington XXX	0	
Round 1	Boldmere St. Michaels	1	Continental Star	0	
Round 1	Bookham	0	Herne Bay	4	
Round 1	Bracknell Town	2	Wodson Park	0	
Round 1	Brading Town	4	St. Francis Rangers	2	
Round 1	Brighouse Town	3	Eccleshill United	3	(aet)
Round 1	Brislington	0	St. Blazey	1	
Round 1	Burnham Ramblers	2	Kentish Town	0	(aet)
Round 1	Cadbury Heath	2	Wootton Bassett Town	1	
Round 1	Calne Town	1	Downton	2	
Round 1	Camberley Town	2	Blackfield & Langley	1	
Round 1	Cambridge Regional College	4	Wellingborough Town	0	
Round 1	Chalfont St. Peter	6	Newbury (2)	0	
Round 1	Clanfield 85	2	Fairford Town	1	
Round 1	Coalville Town	2	Stratford Town	1	
Round 1	Cockfosters	0	Witham Town	3	
Round 1	Colliers Wood United	5	Cove	2	
Round 1	Corinthian	0	Tunbridge Wells	4	
Round 1	Coventry Copsewood	2	Heath Town Rangers	1	
Round 1	Coventry Sphinx	4	Anstey Nomads	3	
Round 1	Crawley Down	0	Rye United	1	
Round 1	Croydon	3	Beckenham Town	7	
Round 1	Dunkirk	2	Blidworth Welfare	0	
Round 1	Dunstable Town	5	AFC Wallingford	0	
Round 1	Dunston UTS	2	Washington	1	
Round 1	Eccleshall	2	Bridgnorth Town	4	
Round 1	Egham Town	2	Molesey	0	
Round 1	Erith & Belvedere	2	Chichester City	1	(aet)
Round 1	Eton Manor	4	FC Clacton	2	
Round 1	Fisher	1	Warlingham	3	
Round 1	Forest Town	3	Greenwood Meadows	1	
Round 1	Formby	2	Flixton	0	
Round 1	Gedling Town	2	Glossop North End	1	
Round 1	Godmanchester Rovers	4	Framlingham Town	0	
Round 1	Gorleston	1	Hadleigh United	0	

Round 1	Guildford City (2)	3	Horley Town	2	(aet)
Round 1	Haringey Borough	1	Tring Athletic	3	
Round 1	Heanor Town	6	Clipstone Welfare	2	
Round 1	Holbrook Sports	4	Arnold Town	4	(aet)
Round 1	Holwell Sports	4	Tividale	3	
Round 1	Ilfracombe Town	1	Hengrove Athletic	2	
Round 1	Ipswich Wanderers	1	Walsham Le Willows	2	
Round 1	Irlam	2	Colne	0	
Round 1	Kidlington	0	Bitton	1	
Round 1	Lancing	1	Christchurch	1	(aet)
Round 1	Langford	1	Hullbridge Sports	3	
Round 1	Leeds Carnegie	4	Easington Colliery	0	
Round 1	Leiston	3	Haverhill Rovers	2	(aet)
Round 1	Leverstock Green	5	Enfield 1893	4	
Round 1	Lordswood	1	Three Bridges	2	
Round 1	Louth Town	3	Barton Town Old Boys	3	
Round 1	Lymington Town	1	Bournemouth (Ams)	2	
Round 1	Maine Road	2	AFC Blackpool	2	(aet)
Round 1	Malvern Town	2	Heather St. Johns	6	
Round 1	Melksham Town	3	Laverstock & Ford	1	
Round 1	Moneyfields	1	Greenwich Borough	0	
Round 1	Newport (IOW)	3	Shoreham	0	
Round 1	Northallerton Town	3	Stokesley	4	
Round 1	Odd Down	7	Bridport	0	
Round 1	Peacehaven & Telscombe	1	Hamble ASSC	0	
Round 1	Ramsbottom United	0	Staveley Miners Welfare	1	
Round 1	Raynes Park Vale	0	Hythe Town	3	
Round 1	Reading Town	4	Newport Pagnell Town	2	
Round 1	Rossendale United	0	Bacup Borough	2	
Round 1	Saltash United	9	Newquay	1	
Round 1	Scarborough Athletic	2	Bridlington Town	2	(aet)
Round 1	Sherborne Town	2	Bodmin Town	2	(aet)
Round 1	South Shields	0	Thackley	2	
Round 1	St. Helens Town	2	Oldham Boro	1	
	Match played at Ashton Town FC				
Round 1	St. Neots Town	11	Felixstowe & Walton United	0	
Round 1	Stansted	2	Takeley	0	
Round 1	Stanway Rovers	4	London APSA	0	
Round 1	Stone Dominoes	1	Heath Hayes	4	
Round 1	Tadcaster Albion	2	Tow Law Town	0	
Round 1	Thrapston Town	2	King's Lynn Town	4	
Round 1	Thurnby Nirvana	1	Shifnal Town	2	
Round 1	Torpoint Athletic	4	Radstock Town	1	
Round 1	Verwood Town	1	Budleigh Salterton	0	(aet)
Round 1	Wantage Town	2	Shrivenham	1	
Round 1	Wednesfield	4	Studley	3	
Round 1	Wellington	5	Tavistock	0	
Round 1	West Auckland Town	6	Birtley Town	0	
Round 1	Whitton United	2	Norwich United	0	
Round 1	Wick	0	VCD Athletic	2	(aet)
Round 1	Willenhall Town	0	Gornal Athletic	2	
Round 1	Winterton Rangers	3	Deeping Rangers	1	

Round 1	Wisbech Town	5	Cogenhoe United	1	
Round 1	Wolverhampton Casuals	1	Bustleholme	3	
Replay	AFC Blackpool	2	Maine Road	1	
Replay	Arnold Town	1	Holbrook Sports	3	
Replay	Barton Town Old Boys	1	Louth Town	0	(aet)
Replay	Bodmin Town	1	Sherborne Town	0	
Replay	Bridlington Town	1	Scarborough Athletic	3	
Replay	Christchurch	0	Lancing	1	
Replay	Eccleshill United	2	Brighouse Town	1	
Replay	Keynsham Town	1	Bishop Sutton	0	
Round 2	AFC Blackpool	0	AFC Liverpool	2	
Round 2	AFC Dunstable	1	Tring Athletic	2	
Round 2	Beckenham Town	2	Peacehaven & Telscombe	1	(aet)
Round 2	Billingham Synthonia	3	Stokesley	1	
Round 2	Bitton	2	Shortwood United	1	
Round 2	Boldmere St. Michaels	1	Gornal Athletic	2	
Round 2	Bootle	1	Shildon	3	
Round 2	Bournemouth (Ams)	5	Odd Down	0	
Round 2	Bridgnorth Town	2	Coalville Town	4	
Round 2	Bristol Manor Farm	3	Torpoint Athletic	7	
Round 2	Bustleholme	2	Barton Town Old Boys	0	
Round 2	Causeway United	2	Gedling Town	0	
Round 2	Chertsey Town	1	Moneyfields	2	
Round 2	Clanfield 85	0	Bemerton Heath Harlequins	3	
Round 2	Colliers Wood United	1	Witney United	0	
	Played at Croydon FC				
Round 2	Coventry Sphinx	0	Dunkirk	3	
Round 2	Dawlish Town	0	Bodmin Town	2	
Round 2	Downton	2	Cadbury Heath	3	
Round 2	Dunstable Town	2	Cambridge Regional College	1	
Round 2	Dunston UTS	4	AFC Emley	0	
Round 2	Eccleshill United	0	Runcorn Town	2	
Round 2	Egham Town	1	Newport (IOW)	2	
Round 2	Epsom & Ewell	4	Bracknell Town	0	
Round 2	Erith & Belvedere	0	Lancing	2	
Round 2	Flackwell Heath	1	Three Bridges	2	
Round 2	Forest Town	0	Tadcaster Albion	4	
Round 2	Formby	1	Bacup Borough	0	
Round 2	Godmanchester Rovers	0	Stanway Rovers	1	
Round 2	Gresley	2	Heanor Town	0	
Round 2	Guildford City	5	Brading Town	2	
Round 2	Heath Hayes	2	Tipton Town	1	
Round 2	Herne Bay	3	Camberley Town	0	
Round 2	Holbrook Sports	7	Holwell Sports	0	
Round 2	Hullbridge Sports	1	Leverstock Green	5	
Round 2	King's Lynn Town	4	Gorleston	0	
Round 2	Kirkley & Pakefield	0	Long Buckby	1	
Round 2	Leeds Carnegie	4	Marske United	3	(aet)
Round 2	New Mills	2	Ashington	4	
Round 2	Norton & Stockton Ancients	4	Irlam	3	
Round 2	Plymouth Parkway	6	Melksham Town	1	

Round 2	Poole Town	4	Wellington	3	
Round 2	Reading Town	1	Warlingham	0	
Round 2	Royston Town	2	Leiston	2	(aet)
Round 2	Rye United	4	Chalfont St. Peter	4	(aet)
	Match played at Sussex County Ground, Lancing				
Round 2	Scarborough Athletic	2	Armthorpe Welfare	2	(aet)
Round 2	Shifnal Town	2	Bloxwich United	2	(aet)
Round 2	St. Blazey	1	Hengrove Athletic	1	(aet)
Round 2	St. Ives Town	2	Aylesbury United	1	
Round 2	St. Neots Town	6	Burnham Ramblers	1	
Round 2	Stansted	3	Eton Manor	1	
Round 2	Staveley Miners Welfare	1	Pickering Town	0	(aet)
Round 2	Stotfold	2	Whitton United	1	
Round 2	Thackley	0	Whitley Bay	1	
Round 2	Tunbridge Wells	8	Holyport	0	
Round 2	VCD Athletic	1	Hythe Town	5	
Round 2	Verwood Town	2	Keynsham Town	1	
Round 2	Wantage Town	3	Binfield	1	
Round 2	Wednesfield	1	Heather St. Johns	3	(aet)
Round 2	West Auckland Town	1	Spennymoor Town	3	
Round 2	Westfields	3	Coventry Copsewood	0	
Round 2	Willand Rovers	2	Saltash United	1	
Round 2	Winterton Rangers	0	St. Helens Town	2	
Round 2	Witham Town	3	Walsham Le Willows	1	
Round 2	Wroxham	4	Wisbech Town	0	
Replay	Armthorpe Welfare	2	Scarborough Athletic	3	
Replay	Bloxwich United	5	Shifnal Town	3	
Replay	Chalfont St. Peter	1	Rye United	2	
Replay	Hengrove Athletic	0	St. Blazey	2	
Replay	Leiston	1	Royston Town	0	
Round 3	Beckenham Town	1	King's Lynn Town	2	
Round 3	Bitton	4	Newport (IOW)	1	
Round 3	Cadbury Heath	4	Reading Town	1	
Round 3	Causeway United	0	Norton & Stockton Ancients	3	
Round 3	Dunkirk	1	Ashington	2	
Round 3	Dunston UTS	2	Heather St. Johns	0	
Round 3	Epsom & Ewell	1	St. Neots Town	2	
Round 3	Formby	2	Tadcaster Albion	3	
Round 3	Gornal Athletic	0	Runcorn Town	3	
Round 3	Gresley	4	Bustleholme	2	
Round 3	Guildford City	4	Moneyfields	3	
Round 3	Heath Hayes	1	Bloxwich United	3	
Round 3	Herne Bay	2	Colliers Wood United	0	
Round 3	Holbrook Sports	4	St. Helens Town	0	
Round 3	Lancing	4	Witham Town	2	(aet)
Round 3	Leeds Carnegie	1	Staveley Miners Welfare	4	
Round 3	Leiston	3	Hythe Town	1	
Round 3	Leverstock Green	3	Tunbridge Wells	1	
Round 3	Plymouth Parkway	1	Bodmin Town	3	(aet)
Round 3	Poole Town	3	Wantage Town	2	
Round 3	Scarborough Athletic	0	Spennymoor Town	3	

Round 3	Shildon	0	Coalville Town	2	
Round 3	St. Blazey	1	Bemerton Heath Harlequins	2	
Round 3	Stanway Rovers	0	Stansted	1	
Round 3	Stotfold	0	Long Buckby	3	
Round 3	Three Bridges	1	Rye United	3	(aet)
Round 3	Tring Athletic	1	Dunstable Town	6	
Round 3	Verwood Town	2	Torpoint Athletic	5	
Round 3	Westfields	1	Billingham Synthonia	2	(aet)
Round 3	Whitley Bay	7	AFC Liverpool	1	
Round 3	Willand Rovers	2	Bournemouth (Ams)	1	
Round 3	Wroxham	0	St. Ives Town	1	(aet)
Round 4	Billingham Synthonia	2	Tadcaster Albion	1	
Round 4	Bitton	2	Coalville Town	3	
Round 4	Bloxwich United	2	Torpoint Athletic	3	
Round 4	Bodmin Town	1	Stansted	4	
Round 4	Cadbury Heath	1	Spennymoor Town	5	
Round 4	Dunstable Town	2	Willand Rovers	0	
Round 4	Gresley	1	St. Neots Town	3	
Round 4	Guildford City	2	Leiston	6	(aet)
Round 4	Herne Bay	1	Whitley Bay	2	
Round 4	Holbrook Sports	2	Lancing	1	
Round 4	Leverstock Green	4	Bemerton Heath Harlequins	1	
Round 4	Long Buckby	3	Ashington	2	
Round 4	Norton & Stockton Ancients	0	King's Lynn Town	1	
Round 4	Poole Town	3	St. Ives Town	2	
Round 4	Runcorn Town	1	Dunston UTS	3	
Round 4	Staveley Miners Welfare	0	Rye United	3	
Round 5	Coalville Town	3	Holbrook Sports	1	(aet)
Round 5	King's Lynn Town	2	St. Neots Town	1	
Round 5	Leiston	2	Long Buckby	1	
Round 5	Leverstock Green	1	Rye United	2	
Round 5	Poole Town	3	Spennymoor Town	2	
Round 5	Stansted	0	Dunston UTS	2	
Round 5	Torpoint Athletic	1	Billingham Synthonia	0	
Round 5	Whitley Bay	5	Dunstable Town	1	
Round 6	Coalville Town	1	Leiston	0	
Round 6	Dunston UTS	1	Whitley Bay	2	
Round 6	King's Lynn Town	3	Rye United	1	(aet)
Round 6	Poole Town	2	Torpoint Athletic	1	
Semi-finals					
1st leg	Coalville Town	3	King's Lynn Town	0	
2nd leg	King's Lynn Town	2	Coalville Town	3	
	Coalville Town won 6-2 on aggregate				
1st leg	Poole Town	1	Whitley Bay	2	
2nd leg	Whitley Bay	3	Poole Town	1	
	Whitley Bay won 5-2 on aggregate				
FINAL	Whitley Bay	3	Coalville Town	2	

ENGLAND INTERNATIONAL LINE-UPS AND STATISTICS 2010

18th June 2010
v ALGERIA (WCF)   Cape Town
D. James	Portsmouth
G. Johnson	Liverpool
A. Cole	Chelsea
S. Gerrard	Liverpool
J. Carragher	Liverpool
J. Terry	Chelsea
A. Lennon	Tottenham H. (sub. S. Wright-Phillips 63)
F. Lampard	Chelsea
E. Heskey	Aston Villa (sub. J. Defoe 74)
W. Rooney	Manchester United
G. Barry	Manchester City (sub. P. Crouch 84)

Result 0-0

23rd June 2010
v SLOVAKIA (WCF)   Port Elizabeth
D. James	Portsmouth
G. Johnson	Liverpool
A. Cole	Chelsea
S. Gerrard	Liverpool
M. Upson	West Ham United
J. Terry	Chelsea
J. Milner	Aston Villa
F. Lampard	Chelsea
J. Defoe	Tottenham H. (sub. E. Heskey 86)
W. Rooney	Manchester United (sub. J. Cole 72)
G. Barry	Manchester City

Result 1-0   Defoe

27th June 2010
v GERMANY (WCF)   Bloemfontein
D. James	Portsmouth
G. Johnson	Liverpool (sub. S. Wright-Phillips 87)
A. Cole	Chelsea
S. Gerrard	Liverpool
M. Upson	West Ham United
J. Terry	Chelsea
J. Milner	Aston Villa (sub. J. Cole 63)
F. Lampard	Chelsea
J. Defoe	Tottenham H. (sub. E. Heskey 71)
W. Rooney	Manchester United
G. Barry	Manchester City

Result 1-4   Upson

11th August 2010
v HUNGARY   Wembley
J. Hart	Manchester City
G. Johnson	Liverpool
A. Cole	Chelsea (sub. K. Gibbs 46)
S. Gerrard	Liverpool (sub. J. Wilshire 82)
P. Jagielka	Everton
J. Terry	Chelsea (sub. M. Dawson 46)
T. Walcott	Arsenal (sub. B. Zamora 46)
F. Lampard	Chelsea (sub. A. Young 46)
A. Johnson	Manchester City
W. Rooney	Manchester Utd. (sub. J. Milner 66)
G. Barry	Manchester City

Result 2-1   Gerrard 2

3rd September 2010
v BULGARIA (ECQ)   Wembley
J. Hart	Manchester City
G. Johnson	Liverpool
A. Cole	Chelsea
S. Gerrard	Liverpool
M. Dawson	Tottenham Hotspur (sub. G. Cahill 57)
P. Jagielka	Everton
T. Walcott	Arsenal (sub. A. Johnson 74)
G. Barry	Manchester City
J. Defoe	Tottenham Hotspur (sub. A. Young 87)
W. Rooney	Manchester United
J. Milner	Manchester City

Result 4-0   Defoe 3, Johnson

7th September 2010
v SWITZERLAND (ECQ)   Basle
J. Hart	Manchester City
G. Johnson	Liverpool
A. Cole	Chelsea
S. Gerrard	Liverpool
J. Lescott	Manchester City
P. Jagielka	Everton
T. Walcott	Arsenal (sub. A. Johnson 13)
G. Barry	Manchester City
J. Defoe	Tottenham Hotspur (sub. D. Bent 70)
W. Rooney	Man. Utd. (sub. S. Wright-Phillips 79)
J. Milner	Manchester City

Result 3-1   Rooney, Johnson, Bent

12th October 2010
v MONTENEGRO (ECQ) *Wembley*

J. Hart	Manchester City
G. Johnson	Liverpool
A. Cole	Chelsea
S. Gerrard	Liverpool
R. Ferdinand	Manchester United
J. Lescott	Manchester City
A. Young	Aston Villa (sub. S. Wright-Phillips 74)
G. Barry	Manchester City
P. Crouch	Tottenham Hotspur (sub. K. Davies 69)
W. Rooney	Manchester United
A. Johnson	Manchester City

Result 0-0

17th November 2010
v FRANCE *Wembley*

B. Foster	Birmingham City
P. Jagielka	Everton
K. Gibbs	Arsenal (sub. S. Warnock 72)
S. Gerrard	Liverpool (sub. P. Crouch 84)
R. Ferdinand	Man. United (sub. M. Richards 46)
J. Lescott	Manchester City
T. Walcott	Arsenal (sub. A. Johnson 46)
J. Henderson	Sunderland
A. Caroll	Newcastle Utd. (sub. J. Bothroyd 72)
G. Barry	Manchester City (sub. A. Young 46)
J. Milner	Manchester City

Result 1-2 Crouch

9th February 2011
v DENMARK *Copenhagen*

J. Hart	Manchester City
G. Johnson	Liverpool
A. Cole	Chelsea (sub. L. Baines 81)
J. Wilshere	Arsenal (sub. G. Barry 46)
M. Dawson	Tottenham Hotspur (sub. G. Cahill 60)
J. Terry	Chelsea
T. Walcott	Arsenal (sub. S. Downing 67)
F. Lampard	Chelsea (sub. S. Parker 46)
D. Bent	Aston Villa
W. Rooney	Manchester Utd. (sub. A. Young 46)
J. Milner	Manchester City

Result 2-1 Bent, Young

26th March 2011
v WALES (ECQ) *Cardiff*

J. Hart	Manchester City
G. Johnson	Liverpool
A. Cole	Chelsea
S. Parker	West Ham Utd. (sub. P. Jagielka 88)
M. Dawson	Tottenham Hotspur
J. Terry	Chelsea
F. Lampard	Chelsea
J. Wilshere	Arsenal (sub. S. Downing 82)
D. Bent	Aston Villa
W. Rooney	Manchester Utd. (sub. J. Milner 70)
A. Young	Aston Villa

Result 2-0 Lampard (pen), Bent

29th March 2011
v GHANA *Wembley*

J. Hart	Manchester City
G. Johnson	Liverpool (sub. J. Lescott 46)
L. Baines	Everton
G. Barry	Manchester City
G. Cahill	Bolton Wanderers
P. Jagielka	Everton
J. Milner	Manchester City
J. Wilshere	Arsenal (sub. M. Jarvis 69)
A. Caroll	Liverpool (sub. J. Defoe 59)
A. Young	Aston Villa (sub. D. Welbeck 81)
S. Downing	Aston Villa

Result 1-1 Carroll

4th June 2011
v SWITZERLAND (ECQ) *Wembley*

J. Hart	Manchester City
G. Johnson	Liverpool
A. Cole	Chelsea (sub. L Baines 30)
S. Parker	West Ham United
R. Ferdinand	Manchester United
J. Terry	Chelsea
T. Walcott	Arsenal (sub. S. Downing 77)
F. Lampard	Chelsea (sub. A. Young 46)
D. Bent	Aston Villa
J. Wilshere	Arsenal
J. Milner	Manchester City

Result 2-2 Lampard (pen), Young

The Evo-Stik Northern Premier League Premier Division 2011/2012 Fixtures

	Ashton United	Bradford Park Avenue	Burscough	Buxton	Chasetown	Chester	Chorley	FC United of Manchester	Frickley Athletic	Hednesford Town	Kendal Town	Marine	Matlock Town	Mickleover Sports	Nantwich Town	North Ferriby United	Northwich Victoria	Rushall Olympic	Stafford Rangers	Stocksbridge Park Steel	Whitby Town	Worksop Town
Ashton United	■	19/11	24/08	28/09	31/03	07/09	17/03	09/04	26/11	10/09	10/12	11/02	13/08	21/04	29/10	25/02	02/01	21/01	08/10	14/01	30/11	27/08
Bradford Park Ave.	24/03	■	27/08	12/11	03/09	15/10	17/12	02/01	14/04	13/08	10/10	21/11	03/12	18/02	21/01	12/09	24/09	09/04	03/03	04/02	14/01	22/08
Burscough	28/01	07/04	■	03/03	21/04	17/08	14/09	24/09	07/01	04/02	29/08	26/12	03/09	24/03	23/11	20/08	12/10	03/12	12/11	18/02	10/12	15/10
Buxton	04/02	31/03	29/10	■	19/11	12/10	21/01	27/08	17/03	14/01	18/02	14/09	09/04	24/09	03/09	03/12	13/08	23/08	10/12	02/01	21/04	23/11
Chasetown	12/11	26/11	17/12	24/03	■	18/02	27/08	21/01	10/09	09/04	24/09	03/03	14/01	06/09	23/08	14/04	29/11	02/01	15/10	11/10	13/08	04/02
Chester	23/11	17/03	14/01	25/02	08/10	■	28/09	24/08	29/10	21/01	14/09	21/04	19/11	10/12	02/01	03/09	09/04	13/08	11/02	27/08	31/03	03/12
Chorley	15/10	21/04	29/11	20/08	07/04	04/02	■	10/09	16/08	24/03	26/12	29/08	18/02	03/03	10/12	07/01	06/09	11/10	28/01	12/11	26/11	24/09
FC United of Manch.	26/12	29/08	11/02	07/04	20/08	28/01	03/12	■	18/02	15/10	23/11	08/10	10/12	12/11	14/09	17/08	21/04	03/09	07/01	03/03	28/09	24/03
Frickley Athletic	03/09	10/12	13/08	15/10	03/12	03/03	14/01	11/10	■	25/02	12/11	24/03	23/08	04/02	27/08	22/11	21/01	24/09	21/04	13/09	02/01	09/04
Hednesford Town	03/12	07/01	27/09	16/08	26/12	20/08	19/11	17/03	08/10	■	07/04	18/02	13/09	28/01	31/03	11/02	10/12	22/11	29/08	03/09	29/10	21/04
Kendal Town	14/04	25/02	02/01	08/10	11/02	29/11	09/04	06/09	31/03	27/08	■	27/09	21/01	26/11	19/11	29/10	14/01	17/03	10/09	17/12	23/08	13/08
Marine	24/09	06/09	09/04	29/11	29/10	17/12	02/01	25/02	19/11	11/10	04/02	■	27/08	10/09	14/01	31/03	23/08	14/04	26/11	13/08	17/03	21/01
Matlock Town	07/01	10/09	26/11	26/12	17/08	24/03	08/10	14/04	28/01	30/11	20/08	07/04	■	29/08	25/02	28/09	03/03	17/12	07/09	15/10	11/02	12/11
Mickleover Sports	17/12	08/10	19/11	11/02	23/11	14/04	29/10	31/03	28/09	24/08	03/09	03/12	02/01	■	14/08	17/03	27/08	14/01	25/02	09/04	21/01	14/09
Nantwich Town	03/03	20/08	06/09	26/11	28/01	29/08	14/04	29/11	07/04	12/11	24/03	16/08	11/10	07/01	■	17/12	15/10	04/02	26/12	24/09	10/09	18/02
North Ferriby United	11/10	29/11	21/01	10/09	10/12	26/11	13/08	14/01	06/09	24/09	03/03	12/11	04/02	15/10	21/04	■	18/02	27/08	24/03	23/08	09/04	02/01
Northwich Victoria	29/08	11/02	25/02	07/01	13/09	26/12	22/11	17/12	20/08	14/04	16/08	28/01	29/10	07/04	17/03	08/10	■	31/03	27/09	03/12	19/11	03/09
Rushall Olympic	20/08	26/12	10/09	28/01	29/08	07/01	25/02	26/11	11/02	06/09	15/10	10/12	21/04	16/08	27/09	07/04	12/11	■	29/11	24/03	08/10	03/03
Stafford Rangers	18/02	29/10	31/03	14/04	17/03	24/09	23/08	13/08	17/12	02/01	03/12	03/09	22/11	11/10	09/04	19/11	04/02	13/09	■	21/01	27/08	14/01
Stocksbridge PS	16/08	27/09	08/10	29/08	25/02	07/04	31/03	29/10	29/11	26/11	21/04	07/01	17/03	26/12	11/02	28/01	10/09	19/11	20/08	■	06/09	10/12
Whitby Town	14/09	17/08	14/04	17/12	07/01	12/11	03/09	04/02	29/08	03/03	28/01	15/10	24/09	20/08	03/12	26/12	24/03	18/02	07/04	23/11	■	12/10
Worksop Town	07/04	28/01	17/03	07/09	28/09	10/09	11/02	19/11	26/12	17/12	07/01	20/08	31/03	30/11	08/10	29/08	26/11	29/10	17/08	14/04	25/02	■

The Evo-Stik Northern Premier League Division One North — 2011/2012 Fixtures

	AFC Fylde	Bamber Bridge	Cammell Laird	Clitheroe	Curzon Ashton	Durham City	Farsley	Garforth	Harrogate Railway Athletic	Lancaster City	Mossley	Ossett Albion	Ossett Town	Preston Cables	Radcliffe Borough	Salford City	Skelmersdale United	Trafford	Wakefield	Warrington Town	Witton Albion	Woodley Sports
AFC Fylde	■	09/04	22/11	21/04	03/12	01/11	15/10	13/08	14/01	02/01	23/08	21/01	25/02	19/11	31/03	11/02	24/09	17/03	27/08	10/12	13/09	29/10
Bamber Bridge	26/12	■	28/01	16/08	24/09	11/02	29/10	25/02	17/03	13/09	22/11	17/12	07/01	01/11	15/10	20/08	29/08	14/04	19/11	03/12	24/03	07/04
Cammell Laird	04/10	13/08	■	01/10	04/02	26/11	12/11	31/03	21/01	23/08	09/04	27/08	03/03	14/01	05/11	29/11	25/10	18/02	17/12	02/01	14/04	10/09
Clitheroe	17/12	14/01	03/12	■	22/11	25/02	24/09	27/08	02/01	09/04	14/04	31/03	01/11	23/08	19/11	29/10	13/09	21/01	13/08	17/03	15/10	11/02
Curzon Ashton	01/10	26/11	29/10	03/10	■	12/11	31/10	21/01	27/08	14/04	02/01	22/08	11/02	17/12	13/08	10/09	03/03	09/04	31/03	14/01	25/02	28/11
Durham City	18/02	25/10	24/09	05/11	17/03	■	13/09	14/01	09/04	22/11	04/02	02/01	15/10	21/01	27/08	19/11	10/12	13/08	23/08	31/03	03/12	21/04
Farsley	10/09	04/02	17/03	26/11	18/02	29/11	■	02/01	25/10	13/08	31/03	04/10	21/04	27/08	14/01	01/10	05/11	23/08	09/04	24/01	19/11	10/12
Garforth	28/01	05/11	07/01	07/04	20/08	16/08	29/08	■	18/02	19/11	13/09	04/02	03/12	17/03	10/12	24/03	21/04	15/10	25/10	24/09	22/11	26/12
Harrogate Rail. Ath.	16/08	12/11	20/08	29/08	07/04	26/12	11/02	01/11	■	24/09	17/12	03/03	13/09	25/02	22/11	07/01	28/01	03/12	14/04	15/10	29/10	24/03
Lancaster City	29/08	29/11	24/03	26/12	10/12	04/10	28/01	03/03	26/11	■	25/10	01/10	20/08	10/09	18/02	16/08	12/11	04/02	05/11	21/04	07/04	07/01
Mossley	24/03	04/10	26/12	10/12	29/08	29/10	07/01	29/11	21/04	11/02	■	10/09	28/01	01/10	17/03	25/02	07/04	19/11	26/11	01/11	16/08	20/08
Ossett Albion	20/08	21/04	07/04	07/01	24/03	29/08	22/11	29/10	19/11	03/12	15/10	■	26/12	11/02	13/09	10/12	16/08	24/09	17/03	25/02	28/01	01/11
Ossett Town	05/11	31/03	19/11	18/02	25/10	10/09	17/12	01/10	29/11	21/01	13/08	09/04	■	14/04	23/08	26/11	04/02	14/01	02/01	27/08	17/03	04/10
Prescot Cables	03/03	18/02	16/08	24/03	21/04	20/08	07/04	12/11	05/11	15/10	03/12	25/10	10/12	■	24/09	29/08	26/12	22/11	04/02	13/09	07/01	28/01
Radcliffe Borough	07/01	10/09	25/02	03/03	28/01	07/04	16/08	14/04	04/10	01/11	12/11	29/11	24/03	26/11	■	26/12	20/08	17/12	01/10	29/10	11/02	29/08
Salford City	25/10	21/01	13/09	04/02	15/10	03/03	03/12	23/08	31/03	14/01	05/11	14/04	24/09	02/01	09/04	■	22/11	27/08	18/02	13/08	17/12	12/11
Skelmersdale Utd.	26/11	02/01	11/02	29/11	19/11	14/04	25/02	17/12	13/08	17/03	27/08	14/01	29/10	09/04	24/01	21/01	■	31/03	10/09	23/08	01/11	01/10
Trafford	12/11	10/12	01/11	20/08	26/12	28/01	24/03	10/09	01/10	29/10	03/03	26/11	16/08	04/10	21/04	07/04	07/01	■	29/11	11/02	29/08	25/02
Wakefield	07/04	03/03	21/04	28/01	07/01	24/03	26/12	11/02	10/12	25/02	24/09	12/11	29/08	29/10	03/12	02/11	15/10	14/09	■	23/11	20/08	17/08
Warrington Town	14/04	01/10	29/08	12/11	16/08	07/01	20/08	26/11	10/09	17/12	18/02	05/11	07/04	29/11	04/02	28/01	24/03	25/10	04/10	■	26/12	03/03
Witton Albion	30/11	24/08	10/12	10/09	05/11	01/10	03/03	05/10	04/02	27/08	14/01	13/08	12/11	31/03	26/10	21/04	18/02	02/01	21/01	09/04	■	26/11
Woodley Sports	04/02	27/08	15/10	25/10	13/09	17/12	14/04	09/04	23/08	31/03	21/01	18/02	22/11	13/08	02/01	17/03	03/12	05/11	14/01	19/11	24/09	■

The Evo-Stik Northern Premier League Division One South 2011/2012 Fixtures

	Belper Town	Brigg Town	Carlton Town	Coalville Town	Goole AFC	Grantham Town	Hucknall Town	Ilkeston	Kidsgrove Athletic	Leek Town	Lincoln United	Loughborough Dynamo	Market Drayton Town	New Mills	Newcastle Town	Quorn	Rainworth Miners Welfare	Romulus	Sheffield FC	Shepshed Dynamo	Stamford	Sutton Coldfield Town
Belper Town	■	16/08	26/11	07/01	04/10	10/09	29/10	29/08	01/10	01/11	24/03	04/02	03/03	21/04	21/01	18/02	20/08	07/04	26/12	17/12	12/11	29/11
Brigg Town	14/01	■	18/02	04/02	09/04	02/01	28/01	17/12	29/10	10/09	04/10	13/08	21/04	31/03	17/03	01/10	19/11	01/11	29/11	23/08	26/11	27/08
Carlton Town	24/09	05/11	■	17/12	21/04	11/02	15/10	23/11	12/11	21/01	29/08	03/12	26/10	03/03	07/01	20/08	26/12	24/03	07/04	14/09	17/08	25/02
Coalville Town	31/03	25/10	14/04	■	28/01	19/11	23/08	25/02	10/12	26/11	10/09	02/01	13/08	27/08	05/11	29/11	11/02	17/03	01/10	14/01	04/10	09/04
Goole AFC	22/11	26/12	10/12	20/08	■	25/02	14/04	21/01	03/03	07/04	16/08	15/10	03/12	12/11	11/02	07/01	13/09	24/09	29/08	25/10	24/03	05/11
Grantham Town	15/10	29/08	29/10	03/03	01/11	■	13/09	21/04	18/02	20/08	21/01	17/12	24/09	04/02	03/12	07/04	16/08	07/01	24/03	22/11	26/12	12/11
Hucknall Town	11/02	20/08	10/09	24/03	17/12	30/11	■	26/12	26/11	17/08	12/11	21/04	05/11	05/10	07/04	03/03	29/08	21/01	07/01	25/02	26/10	01/10
Ilkeston	02/01	14/04	03/10	31/10	13/08	10/12	09/04	■	27/08	04/02	28/11	28/01	22/08	18/02	19/11	10/09	17/03	29/10	26/11	31/03	01/10	14/01
Kidsgrove Athletic	03/12	11/02	17/03	21/04	19/11	05/11	24/09	07/04	■	29/08	20/08	22/11	25/02	17/12	26/12	24/03	07/01	13/09	16/08	15/10	21/01	25/10
Leek Town	25/02	15/10	13/08	24/09	27/08	28/01	14/01	25/10	02/01	■	05/11	31/03	22/11	09/04	13/09	12/11	03/12	17/12	03/03	21/04	11/02	23/08
Lincoln United	23/08	22/11	02/01	15/10	14/01	13/08	17/03	13/09	28/01	18/02	■	27/08	09/04	01/11	10/12	29/10	24/09	03/12	04/02	19/11	14/04	31/03
Loughborough Dyn.	25/10	21/01	01/10	29/08	10/09	14/04	10/12	20/08	04/10	07/01	07/04	■	11/02	26/11	24/03	26/12	25/02	16/08	12/11	05/11	29/11	03/03
Market Drayton T.	19/11	10/12	04/02	21/01	01/10	26/11	18/02	24/03	01/11	04/10	26/12	29/10	■	29/11	29/08	16/08	07/04	20/08	10/09	17/03	07/01	14/04
New Mills	10/12	07/01	19/11	07/04	17/03	24/10	21/11	05/11	14/04	26/12	25/02	24/09	12/09	■	15/08	21/01	24/03	15/10	20/08	03/12	29/08	11/02
Newcastle Town	13/08	12/11	31/03	18/02	29/10	01/10	27/08	03/03	09/04	29/11	21/04	23/08	02/01	14/01	■	26/11	17/12	04/02	01/11	28/01	10/09	04/10
Quorn	05/11	03/12	28/01	13/09	31/03	27/08	19/11	15/10	23/08	17/03	11/02	09/04	14/01	13/08	24/09	■	25/10	22/11	14/04	02/01	25/02	10/12
Rainworth Miners W.	28/01	03/03	09/04	29/10	29/11	14/01	02/01	12/11	31/03	01/10	26/11	01/11	27/08	23/08	14/04	04/02	■	18/02	04/10	13/08	10/12	10/09
Romulus	27/08	25/02	22/08	12/11	26/11	31/03	13/08	11/02	28/11	14/04	01/10	14/01	28/01	10/09	24/10	03/10	05/11	■	10/12	09/04	03/03	02/01
Sheffield FC	09/04	13/09	27/08	03/12	02/01	23/08	31/03	24/09	14/01	19/11	25/10	17/03	15/10	28/01	25/02	17/12	22/11	21/04	■	11/02	05/11	13/08
Shepshed Dynamo	14/04	24/03	30/11	17/08	04/02	05/10	02/11	07/01	10/09	10/12	03/03	18/02	12/11	01/10	20/08	29/08	21/01	26/12	29/10	■	07/04	26/11
Stamford	17/03	24/09	14/01	22/11	23/08	09/04	04/02	03/12	13/08	29/10	17/12	13/09	31/03	02/01	15/10	01/11	21/04	19/11	18/02	27/08	■	28/01
Sutton Coldfield T.	13/09	07/04	01/11	26/12	18/02	17/03	03/12	16/08	04/02	24/03	07/01	19/11	17/12	29/10	22/11	21/04	15/10	29/08	21/01	24/09	20/08	■

978-1-86223-218-1

978-1-86223-204-4

NON-LEAGUE FOOTBALL TABLES
1889 - 2007

978-1-86223-162-7

Football League Tables & Non-League Football Tables

AVAILABLE FROM WWW.SUPPORTERSGUIDES.COM

NON-LEAGUE FOOTBALL TABLES
1889 - 2006

978-1-86223-144-3

978-1-86223-217-4

ALL NON-LEAGUE FOOTBALL TABLES BOOKS FEATURE THE FOLLOWING LEAGUES :

- Isthmian League
- Football Alliance
- Southern League
- Football Conference
- Northern Premier League

ADDITIONAL LEAGUES FEATURED :

- Sussex County League
- The Essex Senior League
- The Northern Counties East League
- The Central League
- The Midland Combination

- Hellenic League
- Midland Combination
- Devon County League

- Western League
- South Western League
- Gloucestershire County League

- United Counties League
- The East Midlands League
- The Welsh Premier League
- The United League
- The Central Amateur League
- The Central Combination
- The Lancashire League
- The Combination

ISBN 978-1-86223-216-7

£9.95

9 781862 232167

Supporters' Guides Series

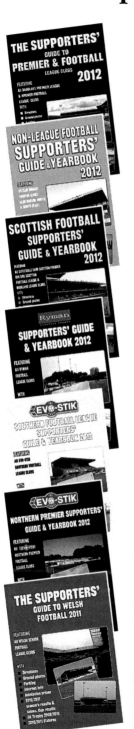

This top-selling series has been published since 1982 and the new editions contain the 2010/2011 Season's results and tables, Directions, Photographs, Telephone numbers, Parking information, Admission details, Disabled information and much more.

THE SUPPORTERS' GUIDE TO PREMIER & FOOTBALL LEAGUE CLUBS 2012

This 28th edition covers all 92 Premiership and Football League clubs. *Price £7.99*

NON-LEAGUE SUPPORTERS' GUIDE AND YEARBOOK 2012

This 20th edition covers all 68 clubs in Step 1 & Step 2 of Non-League football – the Football Conference National, Conference North and Conference South. *Price £7.99*

SCOTTISH FOOTBALL SUPPORTERS' GUIDE AND YEARBOOK 2012

The 19th edition featuring all Scottish Premier League, Scottish League and Highland League clubs. *Price £6.99*

RYMAN FOOTBALL LEAGUE SUPPORTERS' GUIDE AND YEARBOOK 2012

This 2nd edition features the 66 clubs which make up the 3 divisions of the Isthmian League, sponsored by Ryman. *Price £6.99*

THE EVO-STIK LEAGUE SOUTHERN SUPPORTERS' GUIDE AND YEARBOOK 2012

This 2nd edition features the 66 clubs which make up the 3 divisions of the Southern Football League, sponsored by Evo-Stik. *Price £6.99*

THE EVO-STIK NORTHERN PREMIER LEAGUE SUPPORTERS' GUIDE AND YEARBOOK 2012

This 2nd edition features the 67 clubs which make up the 3 divisions of the Northern Premier League, sponsored by Evo-Stik. *Price £6.99*

THE SUPPORTERS' GUIDE TO WELSH FOOTBALL 2011

The enlarged 12th edition covers the 112+ clubs which make up the top 3 tiers of Welsh Football. *Price £8.99*

These books are available UK & Surface post free from –

Soccer Books Limited (Dept. SBL)
72 St. Peter's Avenue
Cleethorpes,   DN35 8HU
United Kingdom